Essays and Dramas

An Inquiry into Passions Engendered by the Idea of Reason

By

Paul C Johnston

Cover photos: Library of Congress

Published by New Atlantic Media,
an imprint of Prosework Media
Chapel Hill, NC
NewAtlanticMedia2002@gmail.com

10 9 8 7 6 5 4 3 2 1

ISBN (paperback) 979-8-9934936-0-2

Printed in the United States of America

Essays and Dramas

An Inquiry into Passions Engendered by the Idea of Reason

CONTENTS

INTRODUCTION

When we European people arrived in North America, we found a Petri dish with plenty of fresh gel, which we set about occupying with the prescience and the foresight of yeast. Life was so good that we began to think that it was because we were exceptional, not because our Petri dish was new, fresh, and big. As a result of thinking ourselves to be exceptional, we did not attend to basic imperatives of the game of life. Instead, we let ourselves lose control of our narratives, then of our territory. The result is that we are now rapidly becoming *not* strangers in a strange land, but strangers in our own land.

We could have respected and worked with nature but chose otherwise. Consequently, nature is working with us via psychopathic leaders and a flood of intruders and aliens. The alternatives we face are stark: re-conquer our own land or fall like a drop of water into an ocean of undifferentiated humanity. How should we proceed? The Iberians provide a model. They set out from Asturias, an enclave in the north, and did not stop until the last Moor was expelled from the peninsula and Al-Andalus became Andalucía. Meanwhile, not far away, on the next peninsula over, an explosion was occurring. The Italians were creating the Europe of the next age. Some of this creation took place at the court of Urbino, which had the reputation of being, of all courts, the most elegant. Castiglione wrote his book on manners while there. Piero della Francesca, while there, wrote his book on perspective in art. Raphael, who came from there, practiced the art of painting with a beauty and ease – with what Castiglione called *sprezzatura* (effortless grace) -- rarely equaled and never surpassed.

Europe produced men of high caliber, the knight and then the gentleman. These men at their best combined contradictory forces, the toughness of Asturias with the manners and elegance of Urbino. The knight was the highest expression of European man. After him came the gentleman, then the citizen, who represented a falling off, but nevertheless had moments of character and substance. After the citizen, decline set it. We Euro men became mass man, and mass man became the coward/bully whose arrival on stage marked the collapse of European masculinity.

The Spanish philosopher, Ortega Y Gasset, makes a distinction between two types of Europeans, Germanic man and Mediterranean man. Germanic man wants to know who he is, where he is, and what he stands for. A Germanic apothecary "cannot grind a mortar and pestle without being clear about how his act fits in with the system of the universe."[1] Mediterranean man is different. His identity is established in relationships with those around him in the plaza. He has no stable identity.

> "It is useless to look to [Mediterranean man] for internal cohesion. He slides through life in a series of discontinuous moments, but if we take in isolation each one of these moments, we are surprised by their grace and spontaneity. ... [This man] is a man of the plaza; he sees a 'you' and a 'him' before he sees himself. ... From this comes his incomparable grace, his psychological astuteness, and his native Machiavellianism." [2]

Nowadays we men of and from Europe fall towards the Mediterranean end of the spectrum (minus the incomparable grace). Fragmentation of community has led to a fragmentation of self.

---

[1] Orgega y Gasset, José *Kant, Hegel, Dilthey*, (Revista de Occidente, Madrid, 1958) p.29. (My translation, as are all quotes from Ortega.)

[2] Ibid, p. 29

We lack internal cohesion. This applies to me, in any case, which is why I aspire to reach the Germanic goal of locating myself in the universe. Falling as I do towards the Mediterranean end of the spectrum, this book cannot help but be a collection of essays, dialogues, dramas, definitions, and letters. What unites the effort is a model that is applied throughout: narrative engenders emotion and emotion issues forth into action.

In addition to the above model, this book is also unified by an agenda. I want us, we men of and from Europe, to change the actions that we take, which to do requires that we change the emotions that we feel, which to do requires that we change the stories that we tell. Finally, this effort is unified by a commitment that I make to myself: say what I think is true. I do not claim that I always -- or even one time -- hit the truth, but I do claim always to be aiming at it.

Essay One

Definitions, Models, and Background

The book *España Invertebrada* came out in 1921. Its author, Ortega y Gasset, said that had there been a book about Spain providing him with insight and orientation, he would have been saved the trouble of constructing badly with scarce materials his own effort, but since the book that he wanted to read did not exist, he felt compelled to write his own. "There are those who can live like sleep walkers," he said, "but I have never succeeded in learning that comfortable manner of existence. I need to live with clear ideas, as wide awake as possible."[3] From the perspective of a century later, his book holds up well, especially if read in conjunction with *The Revolt of the Masses,* written later in the 1920s. In both books Ortega described the appearance of a new man on the stage of European peoples. This man:

> "…is not a representative of a new civilization fighting against an old one. Rather, he is pure negation, effectively a parasite, living on what he denies... for which reason a question has to be asked: what radical deficiency does modern European culture suffer from? The question has to be asked because it is evident that, in the end, from the deficiencies of European culture, there has emerged this type of man now dominant among us." [4]

"What radical deficiency does modern European culture suffer from" is a crucial question to ask. Ortega offers a thoughtful,

---

[3] Ortega y Gasset, José, *España Invertebrada,* (Revista de Occidente, 1961) p.17

[4] Ortega y Gasset, José, *La rebelión de las masas,* (Colección Austral, 25th edition, 1986) p. 205.

sensitive, and clear discussion of this issue, but his work suffers from a defect. Call it the defect of his virtues. He has no model.

The word "model" as used here does not mean a series of statements that lend themselves to being manipulated by the rules of mathematics, but something more basic: it means telling a simple story about a complex story for the purpose of taking action.

Christians would model the deficiency of European culture as a problem involving a people's relationship with divinity. A Marxist would devise a model that sees the deficiency of European culture as a problem emerging out of the class struggle. For Ortega the crucial problem was the rise to dominance of a certain type of human being – a type-man, a mass man – vastly concerned with his own well-being, but not about the people and the disciplines on which his well-being depends. However, as I say, Ortega offers no solution except an improved version of liberal democracy.

In my account the deficiency of our culture has its roots in tensions caused by far history in relation to near history. By far history I mean a repertoire of emotional reactions established in us over the generations of the deep past. By near history I mean the idea of reason. We European peoples assumed that reason would allow us to overcome emotional reactions inherited from the past. This did not happen. Reason has led *not* to our overcoming emotions from the past, but to our expressing these emotions in ways that are catastrophic.

Two actions come out of my model: understand the limits of the idea of reason and tell a different story.

The Unfolding of the Generations

Every species is on a journey from what it was, to what it is, to what it will be if it survives. We human creatures are no exception. Six million years ago (plus or minus a big number) we began diverging from chimpanzees. At one generation per ten years, there are 600,000 generations between us and the chimpanzees. At one generation per twenty years, the number of generations would be 300,000. Whatever the number might be, it is in the range of many hundreds of thousands of generations. Consider a few milestones along the way, measured in terms of generations (at the rate of one per twenty years for purposes of comparison):

* *Australopithecus, a* genus made up of primates of ape-like appearance who walked on two feet. This creature appeared in the fossil record 200,000 generations ago (as always plus or minus a big number).
* *Homo habilis,* a user of tools: 150,000 generations ago.
* *Homo erectus,* up right man: 100,000 generations ago.
* H*omo sapiens,* who we are now. One version, which now may be outdated, has us emerging in Africa 15,000 generations ago and moving north as recently as 3500 generations back. Other versions are more complicated and more controversial. (E.g., *Homo erectus* moves north in waves out of Africa, changes into *Homo neanderthalensis* and *Homo davidensis* as a result of facing the rigors of a cold climate. Later waves of *Homo erectus,* trekking out of Africa, hybridize with the changed versions of themselves and end up as some or as all of us are now. Et cetera.)
* In the range of 500 generations ago our ancestors began making a transition to agriculture.
* No more than 12 to 15 generations ago our ancestors made yet another transition, this time to industrialization.

The purpose of this "model" of human evolution is to draw attention to a point so obvious that it tends to be overlooked: how we make our living now is a recent development.

Human Behavior

(A Simple Story about a Complex Story)

Over hundreds of thousands of generations of hunting and gathering, we creatures in the human line evolved an adaptation that put us at the top of the list in the hierarchy of mammals on planet earth. That adaptation was language. With respect to it I tell a simple story about a complex story. The story comes in the form of three assumptions.

First, over the millennia during which we evolved language, I assume that we established in ourselves a link between language and emotion as follows: we tell stories, these stories engender emotion, and this emotion provides the impulse that sets us in motion. More succinctly: language leads to storytelling, storytelling leads to emotion, and emotion leads to action.

Secondly, I assume that the stories that we hear growing up form our sensibilities. Define the word "sensibility" as a repertoire of emotional reactions to the world around us. Think of sensibility as our most intimate relationship, the one that we have with ourselves. The way that we acquire sensibility is similar to or perhaps identical with the way that we learn to speak our native language. Though other languages can be learned as adults, we are marked forever by our mother tongue. The same happens with sensibility. We can modify or change our sensibilities, but those formed by the dominant stories of our youth mark us for life.

My third assumption about language is that there are areas where we are quick to tell stories, where the stories that we tell are quick to engender emotional reactions, and where the emotional reactions that we feel are quick to issue forth into action. Classify these areas of ready access to story-emotion-action under the heading of the word "proclivity." This too is a complicated area, which, however, I handle in the usual way by telling a simple story about it. My model is that we human creatures have strong proclivities in three areas, classifiable under the heading of them-and-us, high-and-low, and sex. These proclivities are a connection to the past. They are where evolution touches us second by second.

The Pressure of Numbers

One of the driving forces of evolution is the pressure of numbers. What this means – to state the obvious – is that all living creatures, besides having to reproduce themselves generation after generation, have to deal with other members of their own species. This dual task has led to a division of labor -- male and female – which is especially evident among apex predators. The male's job is to protect his particular group from other members of the same species. The female's job is reproduction. Consider lions as an example. Far from being the zebra's enemy, they are essential to the zebra's long-term health and wellbeing. For lions a major problem is other lions. How they manage their relations with each other so as to maintain harmony within the web of life is integral to their success as a species. In the case of lions this is done by dominant males defending territories and by the species having a complex (and from our point of view a severe) strategy of reproduction.

We human creatures do not stand outside of nature. The pressure of numbers has induced us over the millennia to make transitions. A significant one occurred when we climbed down out of the trees and walked out on the plains. Perhaps we did so because life in the trees had become hard, or trees began to thin out, or because out on the plains were unexploited resources. Whatever might have been the case, we hit the jackpot. Becoming comfortably bipedal freed front legs to become arms and hands. Co-ordination to hunt put a premium on communication, which led to language, which in turn led to bigger brains (or vice-versa). Over hundreds of thousands of generations, we became who we now are.

One consequence of our long sojourn as hunter-gatherers was that we had time to catch up with ourselves, so to speak, and achieve a high degree of concordance between our emotions and our strategies for making a living. As an example of this concordance, consider an observation made by Gregory Curtis in a book about cave paintings:

> "The culture that produced the painted caves, despite subtle differences ... lasted almost unchanged for more than 20,000 years. ...
>
> "To last so long this culture must have been deeply satisfying – emotionally, spiritually, intellectually, and practically. It must have engendered and supported a social system that reliably produced and distributed material needs like food, clothing, and shelter. It must have fostered and protected the most basic human relations – friend to friend, man to woman, parent to child – or the society would not have been cohesive enough to survive. ...[5]

Twenty thousand years comes to about thousand generations. As Curtis points out, a complex cultural tradition that is passed down intact through a thousand generations suggests a human community that has solved basic problems of life together. My assumption is that the cave painters were able to maintain a high

---

[5] Curtis, Gregory, ***The Cave Painters*** (Anchor Books, New York) p. 230

degree of continuity across the generations because they were well adapted emotionally to the requirements of their "lifestyle."

Religion and Hunter-Gathering

Shamanism best describes the religion that was believed in during our long sojourn as hunters and gatherers. However, "religion" and "believed in" are somewhat inaccurate terms. If shamanic practice of ancient times resembles shamanic practice of today, no sharp distinctions were made by our ancient ancestors between animals, plants, people, and the spirit world. No separate categories called "religion" and "belief" existed. The idea that daily life and spirit life were separate categories would not have occurred to ancient peoples. Very likely they lived in a world in which emotional connections to everything around them were deep, or could at any moment be suffused with transcendence, danger, connection, mystery, and meaning. Whether or not this was the case there is no way to know. We do know, however, that the stories that our ancient ancestors told to orient themselves worked. For thousands upon thousands of generations, they thrived in the varied, magical (for then), but dangerous place that we now call "nature."

The unbroken cultural tradition of cave painting, which lasted twenty thousand years, is an indication that the cave-painters were well-adapted to the hunting and gathering way of life. Another subtle indication can be noted. One of the clichés about the aboriginal people in America -- some of whom until we came along lived by the ancient pattern of our species -- is that they believed that when they died, they would go to a "happy hunting ground." Think about the implications of this cliché, which I suspect reflects an element of truth. Their idea of heaven was to do in the next life what they were doing in this life. Can any other religious or spiritual tradition make such a claim?

The Transition to Agriculture

Once we – whoever we were then -- climbed down out of the trees and set out across the plains, we opened up a niche that in time came to include most of the land mass of the planet. In this vast new space, we did not feel the pressure of numbers for a long time. However, Mr. Evolution was still on the job. As millennia followed millennia, numbers began to mount, and it became harder for us to find the three- square miles needed *per person* to sustain the hunting way of life. Die back to sustainable levels, find a different way to make a living, or limit our numbers in some other way – such were the alternatives that we faced. We chose the second. Instead of hunting animals and gathering plants, we began raising animals and growing plants, a successful strategy, but one that was replete with problems. A man with emotions shaped over the millennia by the roaming life of a hunter was ill equipped to clear ground, scratch earth, plant seeds, pull weeds, harvest crops -- then go through the same tedious process all over again the following year in the same place. To secure the benefits of the new economy without its drudgery was a desire on the part of all and the achievement of a few.

How?

The short answer: stratification. A slightly longer answer: charismatic leaders turned robust men into warriors and together they reduced weak men to servitude. The strategy worked, but with problems. Because the transition to agriculture was almost instantaneous (in evolutionary terms) we human creatures had not been in the business of farming for a sufficient number of generations to align emotion with action. Our heritage of emotions geared to the hunting life made us unwilling to acquiesce to the confinement and routine of agriculture. Force was necessary to make the agricultural economy work. However, force alone was insufficient. Strongmen die, dissension breaks out among warriors, and successful warriors become soft and are supplanted by hardier groups of men. To achieve stability across the generations required something additional, to wit: a repertoire of narratives telling us who we were, who our gods were, how we reached the place where we found ourselves, who stood high and low among us, and what obligations were owed one to the other. Also of crucial importance: narratives had to persist long enough to shape the sensibilities of the rising generation.

The transition from hunting and gathering to agriculture can be thought of as occurring in three stages. 1) A strongman and his warriors establish a hierarchy by force; 2) a narrative rises to dominance; and 3) the narrative as it is carried from one generation to the next shapes the sensibilities of individuals in their various roles as lord, serf, priest, warrior, woman, and man. A basic assumption of this model is that subordination is not willingly accepted and has to be imposed by force. A second assumption is that force alone is insufficient. Continuity across the generations requires a repertoire of narratives that make the sensibilities of the population complementary. Reducing the model to a formula gives the following: an imposed hierarchy + a dominant story + time (to shape sensibility) = a coherent (stable) social order based on agriculture.

Religion and Agriculture in Europe

The stories that European peoples told as they settled into the agricultural mode of economy first came from the natural religions of Greece, Rome, and Northern Europe, then from Christianity.

These stories shaped the sensibilities of men and women in their various roles in the community. The Christian story --very much part of this process -- was a source of inspiration and creativity in many realms of human endeavor from literature to architecture, to art, to philosophy. Much of the cultural material produced by Christians had the characteristics of a public good, meaning that one person's consumption of the good did not preclude another person's consumption of the same good. Cathedrals, stained glass windows, and sacred music were available to the high but also to the low directly or indirectly. Manners, for example, although originating among the high, were a public good. By filtering down through the gradations of the hierarchy from high to low, they facilitated workable – that is to say, complementary -- relationships among individuals in their various stations in life. The complementarity of relationships that emerged among European peoples was not incidental to the success of the European project. It was the cause of its success.

Ah, but Mr. Evolution had not gone away. He was still on the job.

The Transition to Industrialization

The pressures of a rising population on land and resources, plus the vigor and creativity of European peoples, led to another transition, this time to industrialization, which can be defined as technology + fossil fuel + ideology. (Ideology = stories about politics and economy.)

The transition to industrialization, although monumental in its long-term effects, was at first surprisingly inconsequential, perhaps because industrialization led to a rapid increase in wealth within a population that believed in the Christian religion or that had morals and sensibilities formed by the Christian story. As the narratives of science and ideology became dominant, however, the Christian story lost vitality, especially among the educated, as a result of which the sensibilities of individuals and groups in the population became less and less complementary. Instead of being formed by a single story – Christianity -- the sensibilities of the population came to be formed by different stories. Consider factory owners, for example. Their sensibilities were increasingly formed by stories for and about factory owners (e.g., *The Wealth of Nations*); whereas the sensibilities of factory workers were increasingly formed by stories about factory workers and about those who spoke in their name (e.g., *Das Kapital*). Many of the new political stories that rose to prominence can be classified as variations of a basic core narrative called "contract doctrine."

Contract Doctrine

As Christianity lost vitality, educated men in Europe and in North America began to feel the need for a new narrative on which to establish their social order. They found what they were looking for in the ideas of Hobbes and Locke. These two philosophers told a tidy, logical story about rational human living in the state of nature (a condition of no law, no government, no social order, etc.), who meet, agree on a set of rules, and then establish a government based on the agreed-upon rules. This story had some influence in England during the revolutionary years of the 1640s, when contractarian theory was beginning to take shape. It had a great deal of influence in North America in the late 18th century (when contractarian ideas were imposed on the population in no small measure because such ideas were championed by men of high status in a social order in which men of low status by habit, education, and tradition did not presume to participate). However, the crucial impact of contract doctrine occurred *not* in England in the 1640s nor in North America in the late 18th century, but later, when contract doctrine as a dominant stage-two narrative began to have stage-three effects.

Recall the formula. Stage-one = the imposition of hierarchy; stage-two = the emergence of a dominant narrative; stage-three = the establishment of sensibility in the rising generations based on the dominant narrative. When the dominant stage-two narrative was Christianity, its stage-three effects led to a coherent social order made up of individuals with complementary sensibilities. When the dominant stage-two narrative changed and became contract doctrine, *its* stage-three effects led to fragmentation. Six, seven, eight or more generations had to pass before contractarian stories altered, weakened, or washed out deeply ingrained Christian sensibilities, but it happened. The long-term effect was astonishing. Contract doctrine did NOT to do what it purported to do, i.e., guide people out of a state of nature into civil society, but the opposite. What contract doctrine actually did was take people living in a well-established, stage-three civil society back to nature, that is, back to stage-one, the defining characteristic of which is *what*? Ah, yes, just this: a battle for dominance.

Contract doctrine turned out to be a time bomb introduced into the heart of European civilization. The bomb has exploded. From the perspective of the present day, we can see that an error of understanding lurked at the heart of the contractarian paradigm. Said error was to assume that men in stage-one can deal with each other using stage-three manners. This is essentially incoherent. It is like thinking that you can build a three-story house starting with the third floor.

The Blind Spot of the Founding Fathers

Contract doctrine lies at the heart of the deficiency of our culture. Consider the Founding Fathers of the American Republic as an example. They lived in (what I define as) a stage-three civil society. Because they lived in such a society, they were able to make a transition to a new form of government in North America using civilized methods, i.e., debate, discourse, compromise, agreement, and ballot. They did not know -- and it is hard to see how they could have known -- that changing the rules, customs, and expectations of the game of politics would change the social conditions that produced men like themselves -- but change these conditions they did. The result was that the collective in North American reverted to stage one. It took six, seven, or eight generations to happen, but it did. We (European peoples) are now living out the consequences, by which I mean, we are now pitched into in a stage one battle for dominance. What makes the battle confusing is that it is being fought behind a façade of hollowed out stage-three institutions.

The Battle for Dominance

A stage-one battle is a battle not just to establish dominance over a population, but to establish dominance in the sensibilities of a population. We are in such a battle now. It is not a battle of clan against clan, or of feudal lord against feudal lord, or even of nation against nation, but of type-man against type-man. About this complex process I tell a simple story. My story begins with definitions based on two lines of poetry from *The Second Coming*:

> The best lack all conviction, while the worst
> Are full of passionate intensity..... [6]

The Best (lacking all conviction) and the Worst (full of passionate intensity) are the two type-men in contention. To define these terms, go back to a core assumption of this essay, which is that we

[6] William Butler Yeats, *The Second Coming.*

human beings have various proclivities, one of which is to respond with ready emotion to stories about them-and-us. The people who fall into the category of the Best have this proclivity as we all do. What defines them – i.e., what makes them the so-called Best – is that their sense of who they are, their sense of "us," is formed by stories about family history, communal history, architecture, science, literature, art, philosophy, and religion. The so-designated "Worst," by way of contrast, grow up with a sense of "us" that for historical reasons is not strongly established in their sensibilities by stories about communal history or religion. Rather, the sensibilities of the Worst are formed by cruder, simpler stories. To appreciate the difference between the Best and the Worst, think about the difference between a gang member (a *mafioso* or a member of a criminal cartel), compared to a man who is a traditional patriot. Both type-men are set in motion by stories about us-and-them, but act differently because they have a different understanding of "us" and different emotional reactions based on the different stories that they tell.

In the current, ongoing battle for dominance, the Worst have the advantage. They are "full of passionate intensity." They know what they want – money and power – and act accordingly. Their strategy is the same now as in earlier times. They coil themselves tightly around the interests of a leader. This leader demands control over the men under him, which control the men under him want him to have. They understand that the leader's power over them is the source of their power over everybody else. No laws of man or providence do the Worst scruple to break in order to achieve power and money. Murder, blackmail, ginned up war, bribery, strategies based on deliberate lies -- such are the weapons that they bring to what for them is a stage-one fight for dominance. Think of the Worst as being contemporary with the times as the times now are: six, seven or eight generations after the achievement by contractarian stories of narrative dominance.

In the current ongoing contest for dominance the so-called Best are at a disadvantage. They are not contemporary with the times. They live in a cultural lag. Commerce and politics, they think, have to occur within a framework of rules. Adherence to procedure, coalition-building, amendments to a constitution, reforms carried out within the rules, better candidates, a better distribution of the productivity of the economy -- such are the stories and tactics that the Best bring to the battle for dominance. It is a battle that they are not winning for a reason that is not surprising. The so-called Best think that using knives based on the idea of reason can prevail in a stage-one gun fight for dominance. They are wrong. Life does not work that way. No group of men can be competitive in a contest in which their most competent leaders are killed off by those against whom they are competing.

The Best and the Worse: Who are They?

Roughly speaking, the Best are us, we people of and from Europe. The designation of us as the Best is not as arrogant as it sounds. We are not contemporary with the times, we have let ourselves sink into passivity and confusion, and we refuse to let ourselves see the asymmetric nature of the contest for dominance in which we are pitched. We lack all conviction. As for the Worst, on the other hand, they as type-men first appeared among us (in Western Europe and North America) in mafia gangs and criminal cartels, then they spread to political organizations like the CIA, and now they have metastasized and are taking over more and more institutions. They are full of passionate intensity. To be designated "the

Worst" is not as derogatory as it sounds. The men in this group have power because they are bold enough to grab it.

Conclusions about Contract Doctrine and the Transition from Agriculture to Industry

We, the so-designated Best, are ineffective, passive, and confused. We are not contemporary with the times. We live in a cultural lag. An error of understanding, lurking at the heart of our understanding, is that civilized (stage three) tactics can prevail in a stage one fight for dominance. This failure of understanding on our part goes deep. It is not just that we do not understand what is happening. The problem is that we do not want to understand what is happening.

The Worst, on the other hand, are contemporary with the times, are capable of taking bold actions, and are making a bid to achieve stage-one dominance. How did this change happen? A complicated answer would have to include just about everything that has happened to us, we European peoples, over the last three or four hundred years, including the press of numbers, the rise of science, the productivity of industry, the decline in the vitality of the Christian religion, the loss of first mover advantages due to the diffusion of knowledge, the vast amount of energy from ancient sunlight stored in fossil fuels, et cetera. On the other hand, a simple answer to the question – how did this change happen? – would be to say that an old story, Christianity, was replaced by a new story, contract doctrine, which new story led to fragmentation, which in turn led to social conditions that favored the rise to dominance of tightly linked criminal gangs who then captured the state.

A Few Questions and Answers

If it takes three stages and many generations to go from stage-one to stage-three, what good does it do to understand the process? Maybe we should throw in our lot with the Worst.

We people of and from Europe face various alternatives, three of which come readily to mind. 1) We can hold onto our current ideas about reason and politics. Were we to choose this alternative we would continue bringing inadequate weapons to the ongoing stage-one battle for dominance and lose the battle (as in fact we are losing it now). To lose this battle has somber consequences. Some of us -- the most vigorous, the most courageous, the most moral, the natural leaders -- would be jailed or killed. Most of us would be subordinated, and all of us who survive would see our children absorbed into a big, undifferentiated, demoralized, rootless, easily manipulated, and easily dominated blob of humanity.

2) We can throw in the towel as you suggest. This, however, gains nothing. The outcome would be the same as number one above: the best taken out, the many subordinated, and everybody absorbed.

3) We can resist. We can fight back.

How do we resist?

Tell a different story. Stop basing our definition of "us" on stories about what OUGHT TO BE and start basing our definition of "us" on stories about WHAT IS. My narrative about contract doctrine -- that it leads **not** to the creation of a coherent civil society but to its destruction – is an attempt to take a step in the direction of WHAT IS. I am now going to tell a more filled out version of the story that I am telling now. I call this more filled out version "the Second Synthesis."

The Second Synthesis, with capital letters no less! What does it mean and why is it a second synthesis?

By "synthesis" I mean a story that (in good Hegelian fashion) reconciles contradictory narrative strands. What I call the first synthesis comes from St. Thomas Aquinas and is this: reason complements faith. This first synthesis reconciles the idea of reason with the idea of faith (or you could say, Christianity with Greek philosophy, or Athens with Jerusalem, or even philosophy with history). What I call the Second Synthesis comes from many people, especially Immanuel Kant, and is this: our task is to make the human social world the way it OUGHT TO BE via political activity. This story reconciles present day ideas about equality with proclivities established in us over the millennia of the deep past.

The story that St. Thomas told had a lot of philosophy in it. The story that I am now going to tell you about the Second Synthesis has some philosophy in it, too, but not much compared to St. Thomas.

Essay Two

The Second Synthesis

The Greeks had a word, *logos*, which meant among much else the principle of reasoning in the human mind. The Greeks held the idea in high regard. They were confident that via the logos they could understand the underlying principles that order life. As the centuries rolled along, however, as new narratives began to circulate, as new schools of thought emerged, and, in addition, as the Greek people were hammered by history, they lost their high degree of confidence in themselves and in their ideas.

In time, in the Mediterranean basin, including among the Greeks, a new narrative rose to dominance, called Christianity. Those who believed in the new narrative considered the world to be untrustworthy and saw themselves as unable to deal with it on their own. In that sense they lacked confidence. However, they came to think that help was available from the outside. This help came from God in the form of a task, to wit: make moral choices in the service of ideals as revealed to them by Him in Scripture. Their understanding of this task did not lead to a rejection of the idea of the logos as a special quality of mind, but it caused changes. The early Christian philosopher, St. Augustine, for example, argued that any degree of *ratio* -- of reason -- that a man might deploy was not brought to the table by the man himself, but rather was a gift of God. For St. Augustine, in the words of Ortega y Gasset, "the intuition of truth, of what strictly speaking we call intellect, was the work of God within us. A man in and of himself was not capable of thinking even that 2+2 = 4. [7]

What St. Augustine did was banish reason to a realm above the level of the human. However, from this high place of banishment, the idea of reason as a faculty of mind that a man could deploy on his own account made a long, slow recovery. The place of recovery was medieval Europe. A step on the path of recovery was St. Anselm's *fides quaerens intellectum* (faith seeking understanding). Precisely because St. Anselm believed to the bottom of his heart in the absolute reality of a Trinitarian God, he thought himself to be obligated "to understand as a natural man all that was vouchsafed to him supernaturally through revelation."[8] Compared to St. Augustine, who had set man's natural reasoning abilities equal to zero, Anselm represented an increase in confidence. A man

---

[7] Ortega y Gasset, José. *Obras Completas*, 1983 Tomo V, *p.127*
[8] Ortega y Gasset, José, *Obras Completas*, 1983, Tomo V, p. 127

could trust himself a bit and use his natural powers of reason to try to understand the gift of revelation. The attempt to do so, to understand the great gift of revelation, was scholastic theology.

The recovery of confidence in the idea of reason continued with St. Thomas Aquinas. God Himself -- St. Thomas argued -- in the act of being Himself, makes the world rational. [9] What this means is that God's reasoning powers and man's reasoning powers are the same, hence logic for both are the same. However, differences exist. Unaided reason cannot go as far as it has to go in order to know how to live correctly in the world. Aristotle, for example, the best of the ancients, was able to draw valid conclusions, such as, for example, that there had to be a God. However, Aristotle's concept of deity was remote and abstract, a logical necessity, a first mover in the chain of causation and nothing more. According to St. Thomas, to live correctly in the world requires additional knowledge, but additional knowledge lies beyond the reach even of men with the mental powers of Aristotle. Knowledge about how to live correctly in the world requires a turn to Scripture, by means of which God Himself reveals details about Himself and His intentions. Scripture in this way fills out and extends man's reliable but limited faculties of reason.

The conclusion that St. Thomas drew was that reason does not contradict faith. Rather, **reason complements faith.** This was powerful. Call it the first great European synthesis, an oversimplification to be sure, but nevertheless useful. Via this formula St. Thomas reconciled Greek philosophy with sacred scripture and provided the intellectual foundation of Western European culture for centuries to come and in the case of Catholic Christianity, even until recent times.

---

[9] Ibid. 132

Although both profound and successful, this first great intellectual synthesis did not go unchallenged. Not long after having been worked out, it was shaken by Duns Scotus, a man or perhaps a school of men. God exists beyond logic, this school argued. To say that God has to be rational is to subordinate Him to logic and make Him small. Even to say that God's existence is necessary takes away God's freedom by imposing upon Him the greatest of all obligations, the obligation to be. This is error. Ortega described the position of Duns Scotus as follows: "God is pure willpower ... before all else that exists including reason... The existence of reason is a fact not a principle. In His true being, God is irrational and beyond all intelligence."[10] More succinct than Ortega or Duns Scotus is the Book of Exodus where God says to Moses: *"I am that I am."* [Exodus 3:14]

Duns Scotus turned the scholastic tradition upside down and contributed to -- and was a symptom of -- a crisis among European peoples that was unlike the crisis of ancient times. In ancient times men fell into a state of doubt about themselves. In the crisis of the late medieval period, (Western European) men came to harbor doubts about their Church.

Duns Scotus was a symptom of change soon visible everywhere in Catholic Europe. Instead of contemplating God, men of the late medieval period turned their gaze in the direction of the world. As an example of this change consider a new monastic order that arose in Spain, the Jesuits, compared to an earlier order, the Augustinians. The strategy of the Augustinians was to retire from the world in order to contemplate the more perfect City of God, or, in Ortega's words, in order to stand with their faces to God and their backs to the world. By way of comparison, the

---

[10] Ibid.132

Jesuits stood with their backs to God and to the great weight of medieval Christianity and turned their gaze in the direction of the world. The job of the Jesuits, as they saw it, was to fight for a beleaguered Church in just those places where the world was most dense: politics, legal establishments, and educational institutions.[11]

Movement away from contemplating the perfection of the divine order towards engagement with the world occurred in another crucial dimension as well. A small group of Europeans began to apply the idea of reason to the investigation of nature, a change not as radical as at first might be supposed. (If Scripture complements man's reliable but limited ability to reason, then investigation of God's work -- i.e. of nature -- should confirm the majesty of God's word.) This small number of men from various parts of Europe started down a new path and met with success along the way. Their success led to an increase in confidence, which in their case was confidence in the idea of reason. As an idea it became less limited, less insufficient, less dependent upon a complementary backup revelation from God (as per St Thomas), and more reliable as a faculty of mind capable of being deployed in its own right. The men of this new current in European thought were surprisingly close to St Thomas, with, however, a key difference. God no longer occupied the foreground of their worldview. Rather, instead, God retired into the background while still yet nevertheless generously leaving behind His handiwork in the form of a rational universe.

What these men did was turn the idea of reason into belief.

The classical expression of confidence in reason, and in what came to be known as rationality, was provided by Descartes, who put into words the narrative at the core of the new vision: **clear ideas clearly linked together lead to truth.** Out of this new vision

[11] Ibid.156

came science, especially physics, the discipline at the heart of the western, secular, intellectual tradition.

Christianity continued to occupy the vital core of the pious people of Europe, but not of the brilliant, the alert, the curious, and the agitated. These more restless souls were drawn to the idea of reason as a unique faculty of mind and remained loyal to the idea even as it took them in a direction that seemed not to confirm the majesty of God's word. Rather the opposite. Their investigation of the idea of reason in relation to the processes of nature sent wave upon wave rolling across the surface of life and crashing into the bulwark of Christianity in the form of an unfolding, expanding, successful, ever-encroaching narrative about the possibilities and potentialities of the rational mind.

Europeans on the new path of reason soon began drawing up philosophical maps. They wanted to do what peoples everywhere have to do: locate themselves in the world. In their case this meant reconciling the two most important landmarks on the European horizon, the same two as always, Athens and Jerusalem, reason and faith, the expanding belief in reason and the deeply rooted Christian tradition.

For the scholars of the medieval period no doubts existed about orders of rank. God stood over Aristotle, Christianity stood over Greek paganism, and revelation stood over reason. By the 17th and 18th centuries, however, the situation had changed. Reconciliation of faith and reason meant understanding the status and reliability of knowledge about God in light of the standards of discourse that had arisen within the European philosophical tradition. To say this as succinctly as possible, reconciliation by the 17th and certainly by the 18th century meant that the queen herself (theology) had to obey the law (rationality). Implicit in this process was the reversal of a crucial order of rank, not revelation over reason but the other way around, reason over revelation.

However, the problem of reconciliation turned out to be more complicated than just making sure that the queen obeyed the law. Though promising much, delivering much, and at every turn in the road opening up vistas of new and expanding possibility, reason had its own dangers and these began to appear.

David Hume, when he arrived on the scene, wanted to determine the status and reliability of statements such as "I believe in God." The verbal formula used here to convey this point is to say that Hume wanted to make sure that the medieval queen of the sciences, theology, was obeying the laws of logic. However, Hume's inquiry, which began with theology, did not end with theology. In the process of trying to get the queen to obey the law, another problem arose: getting the law to obey the law, i.e., grounding rationality in arguments themselves rigorously rational. In his attempt to determine the rational foundations of the idea of reason, Hume was looking for arguments to which all men would be compelled to agree by the force of "clear ideas clearly linked together." This he was unable to do. Essential links in the sequence of discourse on which depended the idea of rationality could not be reduced to "clear ideas clearly linked together." The foundations of rationality seemed to involve matters of habit, history, experience, and faith that were non-rational, that lay beyond us.

(In particular Hume could not see how causality, an idea crucial to the rational project, was necessary. Our understanding of causality seemed to depend on experience rather than on logic. Heat, for example, *causes* water to boil. This we know. However, in the end, in the final analysis, we do not know why. In terms of basic, down in the dirt, hard core logic, we do not know whether or not heat will cause water to boil tomorrow. Our knowledge that heat causes water to boil depends entirely upon experience.)

Cracks in the foundation on which rested the idea of rationality were a problem for Immanuel Kant. He sensed threats to a tradition of discourse that promised much in the way of control, comfort, order, safety, and avoidance of conflict. His response was to march onto the battlefield of philosophy, famously awakened by Hume from "dogmatic slumbers," determined to set matters right.

Kant's strategy was to retreat in some areas while advancing in others. The solutions that he came up with lie at the heart of what I call the Second Synthesis, and therefore at the heart of the crisis of the present age. On the side of retreat, Kant argued that we do not know the world directly because we do not receive raw data from it. Rather, we structure incoming data using mental categories that we ourselves bring to the act of perception. These structuring categories – which Kant called "necessary conditions for the possibility of experience" -- boil down to three: time, space, and cause-and-effect. Because we structure the world in the act of perceiving the world, we can be confident that systems of thought based only on experience are true.

Kant's argument at this point is bold but nevertheless represents metaphysical retreat. He leaves important issues unresolved and un-resolvable, such as, for example, a rational proof for the existence of God. (St. Thomas had argued that the idea of God -- as first mover, as uncaused cause -- lay within the grasp of natural reason, because natural reason tells us that there has to be a starting point at some moment in the past. No, not so, answered Kant. Reason tells us no such thing. We have no experience of the beginning of time and cannot apply our categories of thought to matters beyond experience. The universe could be finite and have a first cause, or the universe could be infinite and go back through an endless series of causes. We cannot resolve this issue by pure reason.)

However, while Kant's argument at this point represents retreat, the retreat is tactical. A place exists where Kant does not retreat. That place is morality. He argues that the basis of morality is the categorical imperative. ("...so act that the maxim of your will could always hold at the same time as a principle establishing universal law.")[12] What makes the categorical imperative rational is that it is form, not content. (Should I do X, no matter what X might be? Apply the categorical imperative: what would happen if everybody did X?) Here Kant makes his stand and holds his ground. Our knowledge of the moral law is rational, therefore secure. Not only can we know the moral law, we can act on it based on nothing more than our rational comprehension of it. To use highfalutin language, Kant proclaims **the autonomy of the moral will.**[13] This is crucial. Because our moral will is autonomous, we stand outside the chain of causation and are able to act in the world based on reason, that is, on what Kant calls practical reason. (Practical reason = human action = what is made real by our will.)

With the idea of practical reason, Kant is off to the races. Since our moral will is unconditioned, our moral duty is to act on the highest moral position that we can attain as a rational being. The highest moral position that we can attain is to believe in God. Pure reason cannot tell us that there is a God, but neither can it tell us that there is no God. Where this leaves us is as follows: we have a moral duty to believe in God[14] (as well as two other basic supports of morality: freedom and immortality, reached by a similar argument.)

---

[12] Kant,I. *The Critique of Practical Reason (*Bobbs-Merrill Co. translated by Lewis Beck White*)* p. 30

[13] Kant, I. Ibid. p. 117

[14] Kant, I Ibid, p. 130

The Spanish philosophers, Miguel de Unamuno and Jose Ortega y Gasset, were skeptical. Unamuno took Kant's argument to be one in which, to secure belief in the immortality of his soul, Kant reconstructs in *The Critique of Practical Reason* what he abolished in *The Critique of Pure Reason.* [15] As for Ortega, he thought that in the basement, in the place of final accounting, where contact is made with bedrock, Kant's philosophy did not rest upon an acceptance of WHAT IS but rather upon *yo quiero* ("I want").

Here is how Ortega put it:

> "I don't think that in all of human history has anyone pulled off a more daring inversion. Kant called this his "Copernican feat." But in truth it is much more. Copernicus limited himself to changing one reality for another at the center of the cosmos. Kant set himself against all of reality. ... To know is not to copy, but, on the contrary, to know is to decree. ... To know is not to see, but to command. ...
>
> We Mediterranean people and therefore contemplatives will always be left stupefied seeing how Kant, instead of asking himself: how must I think in order that my thoughts fit reality, instead asks the opposite question: how does reality have to be in order for knowledge to be possible....
>
> Here we have what I call the philosophy of the Viking. When to ***what is*** you openly oppose what ***ought to be,*** we suspect always that hidden behind this is a human, all too human, I want. [16]

---

[15] de Unamuno, Miguel, *Tragic Sense of Life,* Dover Publications, 1954 edition, translated by J.E. Crawford Flitch. P 3

[16] Ortega y Gasset, José, *Prólogo para Alemanes* section 4, introduction to the German edition of *El tema de nuestro tiempo.*

Kant's Copernican feat actually involves two summersaults. 1) To guarantee that knowledge based on experience is valid, he flips something on the outside -- time, space, and cause-and-effect -- to the inside by putting these categories inside the human mind. 2) To guarantee that following the moral law is rational, he flips something on the inside, our moral will, to the outside by making it into a God, who, although we cannot prove by pure reason that He exists – or does not exist -- we can act based on a moral system in which belief in His existence is a duty backed by the high authority of the idea of reason.

The first summersault does not change much. Whether we consider space and time to be on the inside or on the outside, we continue to perceive the world about the same as always. The second summersault, on the other hand, is a different kettle of fish.

Because knowledge of the moral law is rational, it is secure. Because it is secure it is possible to know with confidence what should be done. To know with confidence what should be done means that it is possible for **me** to know with confidence what **you** should do and what **we** together should do. Now throw in one more consideration. "To put space and time inside man is to put man outside of space and time." [17] To be outside of space and time is to be outside of nature. To be outside of nature is to be not limited by natural processes. To be not limited by natural processes – and to have a moral will that is autonomous -- means that nothing stops us from making the human community the way it OUGHT TO BE.

Kant and the History of an Idea

The Greeks invented the idea of reason and naively assumed that it was a faculty of mind that gave them access to the world the

[17] Ortega y Gasset, José. *La rebelión de las masas* p. 38

way it is. They might make errors, but these errors were personal not structural. St. Augustine came along and placed reason in the realm of the divine. Next medieval and post-medieval European scholars brought reason back down to earth by once again making it a faculty not above us but in us. David Hume, when he arrived on stage, began deconstructing the idea of reason. His work threatened to cause the idea to evaporate. Kant, riding to the rescue, agreed with St. Augustine that reason was special. The boldness of the step that Kant took was NOT to try to pull reason down to earth to be with us at our level, but rather, to salvage the idea of reason by giving to us a task: use reason itself to elevate ourselves to *its* level, that is, use reason to make the human world the way it OUGHT TO BE.

The injunction to use reason to make the human world the way it OUGHT TO BE lies at the core of the story that I call "the Second Synthesis." However, two ideas from the contractarian philosophical tradition have to be added to the story, the idea of the individual and the idea of rational self-interest in politics.

Contributions of the Contractarian Philosophical Tradition to the Second Synthesis

In medieval times a school of philosophy called "contractarianism" concerned itself with the obligations that the various strata of society owed to each other, e.g., what the nobility owed to commoners, what commoners owed to the nobles, what both owned to the clergy, and so forth. However, in the 17th century, contract doctrine underwent a change of fortune. First Thomas Hobbes then John Locke used the ideas of the contractarian school as intellectual weapons in a long running conflict in England between the institution of the crown and the institution of the parliament, curiously enough one to bolster and the other to oppose royal authority. In resorting to the ideas of the contractarian school both men shifted the emphasis away from collective categories (groups, estates, guilds) and instead placed it upon the individual, thereby making the idea of the individual a central concept around which they constructed their philosophical narratives.

In their reworked version of the contractarian story, both Hobbes and Locke start with the idea of a man considered to be separate and alone in a state of nature. Acting in his own self-interest, this man agrees with other men also in the state of nature to establish an all-powerful sovereign (Hobbes) or a legislative assembly (Locke).

These narratives about the state of nature allowed contractarian philosophers to base their descriptions of political activity on the idea of reason -- in the form of the rational self-interest of the individual -- rather than on narratives about hereditary rights or divine will. However, the process by which the idea of the individual actually became incorporated into the narrative that I call the Second Synthesis went powerfully in a contrary direction. The re-worked contractarian story turned the individual into a "fundamental unit of account" and into a "court of last appeal," that is, into a standard by which to judge the moral worth of social arrangements and political outcomes, e.g.:

1) Political authority. Because the individual is the fundamental unit of account, the purpose of political institutions is to further the aims and interests of the individual. Groups exist for the individual, not the other way around. Political limitations upon individuals, to be fully moral, have to be agreed to by the individual at some level in some way. That is, all political constraints to be legitimate have to be self-imposed.

2) Self-Interest. Because the individual is the fundamental unit of account, the desires of the individual are legitimate as long as they are realized within the bounds of the rules.
3) Equality. Because the individual is the fundamental unit of account, no inherent reason exists why one individual should count more than another. Privileges of birth, tradition, caste, class, race, region or any other non-individual category have no inherent moral standing.

Add these contractarian ideas (about rational self-interest in politics and the idea of the individual) to Kant's narrative about the autonomy of the moral will and what you get is the Second Synthesis.

The Second Synthesis Described

*We are rational beings who can know what is moral.

*Because we are rational, we can with confidence know that certain states of the world OUGHT TO BE.

* We move ourselves collectively from where we are to where we OUGHT TO BE via pursuit of our rational self-interest in the political arena.

* A standard exists by which to judge the value of political outcomes: the idea of the individual.

The Second Synthesis Defined

Our task is to make the human world -- via political activity -- the way it OUGHT TO BE.

What Kant and the Contractaian Philosophers Accomplished

The rise to dominance of the Second Synthesis did not change a task located at the heart of Euro-Christian civilization. Said task – make moral choices in the service of ideals -- goes all the way back to early Christian times. What the Second Synthesis did was change **who has the authority to define ideals**. Under the old Christian dispensation this authority resided with the custodians of the word of God, i.e., the Church, and also with those elevated by God to positions of high degree, i.e., the king. In the new dispensation of the Second Synthesis, the authority to define ideals came to reside with participants in the political arena. What this meant is that the great weight of Christian moral seriousness -- hitherto mobilized by Cross and Crown – instead came to be mobilized by political agents seeking political power in the political arena. To say the change was important would be an understatement. Explosions caused by the change are still reverberating. Second Synthesis stories have had a vast influence upon human activity, which leads to a question: how does the process work? How do ideas influence behavior?

How Ideas Influence Human Behavior: a Model

The process by which ideas influence behavior is complex, obviously, which means: 1) many stories can be told about how the process works, and 2) one's model cannot be separated from one's purpose. With these limitations in mind, let me tell a simple story about a complex story, that is, let me devise a model about how ideas influence human behavior.

Ortega y Gasset in *History as System* makes the observation that human beings do not have a nature; rather, they only have history. Can this be right? Is it not possible to say that all human beings share traits in common, such as, for example, all human beings feel emotion? Given the universality of emotion, is it possible to tell a story about how emotions and ideas are linked? My answer is "yes," it is possible. I devise a model based on six statements:

1) Human beings have emotional reactions.

2) These emotional reactions are triggered -- are *engendered* -- by stories.
3) Stories are ideas and ideas are stories. That is, in my model the word "idea" and word "story" are different manifestations of the same basic, narrative phenomenon. An idea is a condensed story.
4) Dominant stories establish or form the sensibilities of the next generation.
5) Emotional reactions engendered by stories lead to action.
6) Within the category of telling stories, feeling emotions, and taking action three areas stand out. Classify these areas under the heading of them-and-us, high-and-low, and sex.

That's it. That's the model. It is about how people link themselves together horizontally, vertically, and sexually by telling stories that engender emotions that in turn issue forth into action. (The model is also about how the dominant narratives of one generation form the sensibilities of the next generation). To crank the model, begin with the word "us" (or its equivalent in other languages, obviously). Stories using this word engender feelings that lead to the action of forming clans, tribes, clubs, communities, nations, etc. People not in the category of "us" fall implicitly or explicitly into the category of "them." Competition between "us" and "them" arises and enhances feelings of attraction towards 'us' and of antipathy towards 'them."

Once human beings start thinking of themselves as an "us," they become sensitive to gradations of rank, and start telling stories about who has high rank and who does not. Stories about rank engender a desire to reach a position of high rank within one's understanding of "us," an outcome achieved by success with respect to prevailing measures of success (land, money, ancestors, valor in battle, servants, children, artistic talent, spiritual depth, et cetera). High social standing leads to confidence, and confidence is intimately connected to a third great emotional aspect of human life together: sex. Those with high rank are more likely to be confident, and those who are confident are more likely to secure a mate, or a mate of higher quality, or more mates, or a mate of higher quality for one's offspring -- or some or all of the above.

About this model, give it a name, "Cunning Nature," and a gender, "She." Understand that She has three commandments for Her human creatures: 1) form an "us;" 2) strive to gain altitude within your "us;" and 3) go forth and multiply with the highest quality mate that you can link yourself to. These commandments lead to the playing of the game of life, but they also do something else that is even more fundamental. They create the game that is being played, which game is actually rather in the way of being difficult. To give it a name, call it "evolution." To get Her creatures to be willing to endure -- and ultimately to love -- the rigors of the game of life is the cunning of Cunning Nature.

Application of the above Model of Human Behavior to the Ideas of the Second Synthesis

Scribblers, visionaries, saints, frauds, hacks, idealists, manipulators, cynics, monsters -- the best and the worst that European humanity had to offer -- used the ideas of the Second Synthesis to tell stories, some sensible and practical, some more religious than political, some with apocalyptic overtones, but all, however, revolving around a single, great theme: *this* arrangement, *this* set of laws, *this* practice, *this* economic system, *this* condition, *this* outcome is how human life together OUGHT TO BE.

Consider the following quote from a well-known source:

> "The history of all hitherto existing society is the history of class struggles. ... The modern bourgeois society that has sprouted from the ruins of feudal society has not done away with class antagonisms. ... Society as a whole is more and more splitting up into two great hostile camps, into two great classes directly facing each other—bourgeoisie and proletariat..."

This fragment (from the *Communist Manifesto* need I say) is an example of a Second Synthesis story that burst upon the scene in 19th century Europe. It and many other stories led people to form into groups and then to march behind banners proclaiming sentiments such as "workers of the world, unite." The people marching behind these banners were new players on the stage of European politics. However, the game that they were playing was not new. It was the same game as always being played by the same rules as always: coalesce into an "us" and compete against "them."

Second Synthesis Stories

Classify Second Synthesis stories -- and the vast amount of political activity set in motion by them -- under the heading of the word "socialism." By this I do not mean just those who want the government to have a greater hand in the means of production (this I call "classical socialism.") Rather, by "socialism" I mean all attempts to achieve Second Synthesis OUGHT TO BE outcomes via collective activity, i.e. via politics. Crucial to understand about socialism is that it gave to European peoples a way to accomplish contradictory goals. On the one hand they could embrace ideas about equality. On the other hand, they could establish essential categories necessary for playing the game of life, i.e., them-and-us and high-and-low.

Socialism achieved this contradictory outcome:

1) by positing ideals;
2) by using ideals to create bad guys and good guys, and
3) by forming a political coalition of good guys for the purpose of using the power of the state to help the good guy and hurt the bad guy.

Take these steps in order. (In parentheses I will say a word or two about near history or far history or both.)

Step 1) Posit ideals, that is, decree states of the world that OUGHT TO BE, such as: *liberté, égalité, fraternité*, a classless society, careers open to talent, equal pay for equal work, from each according to his capacity to each according to his need, equality under the law, men judged not by the color of their skin but by the content of their character, a level playing field, one man/one vote, a tobacco-free society, no child left behind, etc.

(Step one reflects Kant's assumptions about the autonomy of the moral will. An outcome that is rational – i.e., not internally contradictory -- can be achieved by engagement of the moral will. Although it would be inaccurate to say that Kant caused socialism, it would be more than accurate to say that he made important contributions to a process whereby European peoples came to think that they enjoyed great latitude with respect to what could be accomplished in the political arena. Amazing, even stunning, is the degree of penetration of Kant's narrative. The whole of contemporary politics is mediated by the idea of OUGHT TO BE, yet at the same time there is little understanding of the costs that are involved.)

Step 2) Define bad guys and good guys. The bad guys are those who stand in the way of realizing the ideal. Consider, for example, the factory owner of classical Marxism. He wants to exploit his workers by stealing their labor. His greed stands in the way of realizing the ideal of a classless society. This makes him bad. Because he is bad, he is one of "them." Because he is one of "them" he is okay to hate. On the other hand, the workers being exploited by the factory owner -- and those who stand in solidarity with the workers -- are good. They strive to realize the ideal of equality. They are "us."

(Once again notice how bits of Kant's narrative are woven into the fabric of political discourse. Because we can know what OUGHT TO BE, we can know that those who stand in the way of what OUGHT TO BE are immoral, i.e., bad, i.e., "them.")

Step 3) Form a political coalition made up of good guys and use this coalition to acquire state power in the name of using the power of the state to undo the bad of the bad guy and move society closer to where it OUGHT TO BE.

(With this step European man finds a way to comply with another of Mother Nature's great injunctions: achieve high social standing among "us." Government is the vehicle that makes it possible for an individual to achieve high social standing within a group of men and women who are set in motion by stories about equality.)

The great accomplishment of socialism was to give European peoples a way to believe in equality while at the same time giving the ambitions and the energetic among them a way to play the game of life. What makes socialism operational in day-to-day politics is the idea of the victim.

Many Victims, One Victimizer

First on stage in the 19th century as a victim were factory workers. They were victims of a greedy factory owner who was stealing their labor. In the decades that followed many other people came to be classified as victims: Africans, women, poor people in general, people in other countries (victims of imperialism), cigarette smokers, homosexuals, children left behind, etc.

The existence of victims implies the existence of a victimizer, which leads to a question: who has played the role of victimizer over the generations? Here matters are different. Here from beginning to end only one group has played the role of victimizer: males of European origin, that is to say, white men. This has consequences. So conditioned by Second Synthesis narratives are we men (of and from Europe) that we now are comfortable linking ourselves together politically **only** in the name of pursuing abstract goals such as democracy, equality, the greatest good to the greatest number, or in the name of helping people who are victims (blacks, women, foreign victims of imperialism, etc.). Appeals made to us as "white men" arouse emotions of suspicion **in us** and engender **in us** an emotional reaction of discomfort and distress. The term "white man" is so toxic that we white men have succumbed to a sickness. To give this sickness a name, call it "social lupus".

"Lupus" (which means wolf in Latin) is now the name of a disease of autoimmunity in which a person becomes allergic to himself or herself. Something similar has happened to us, we men of European origin. Stories about white men acting in their own self-interest engender in us – in we white men -- NOT favorable emotions associated with "us," but unfavorable emotions associated with "them." We have become allergic to ourselves and are now wolves who auto-consume. This has an effect that is devastating. Our leaders base their moral claim to power on support of victims and on opposition to victimizers. Since the victimizer is always a "white man," our own leaders end up **not** identifying with us as a people. On the contrary, in their minds, for us white men to pursue our interests as a group is racism. A curious consequence of this process is that the first victims on the list of victims – white European proletarians – have now been delisted.

That we have succumbed to this autoimmune disorder suggests a truth about Cunning Nature. She demands that we organize ourselves into clumps of them-and-us and She gets what She demands even if, to give Her what She wants, we have to turn ourselves into a "them" and consume ourselves.

The Definition of Socialism

Socialism is a doctrine that makes it possible to accomplish a contradictory task: believe in equality, but also establish two essential categories needed to play the game of life, them-and-us and high-and-low.

The Strategy of Socialism

*Use the implicitly sunny assumptions of Second Synthesis narratives to paint a picture of how society OUGHT TO BE.

*Define the task of government as making society the way it OUGHT TO BE.

*Compare flawed existing governments run by flesh and blood people to unflawed theoretical governments described in books, pamphlets, and tracts.

*Define those who support flawed, actually existing governments as "them," and those who support unflawed theoretical governments as "us."

*In what has to be seen as a stroke of pure political genius on the part of classical socialism, after gaining political power, judge yourselves not by what you did to get power or what you do to keep power. Instead, stand on the high ground of the noble aspirations of your ideology, that is, judge yourselves *not* by your actions or by your results, but by your intentions.

The Cost of Socialism

The drama of socialism reconciles emotional proclivities inherited from the far past (them-and-us, and high-and-low) with contemporary ideals (equality, above all). There is a cost to this reconciliation.

1) Socialism does not recognize European men (i.e. us, we white men) as a legitimate group with legitimate interests. As a result, we European men fail to hold a key conversation among ourselves: what is in our interest as a people? To feel uncomfortable discussing our interests as a people leaves us impaired when it comes to finding ways to protect ourselves in the political arena. We are especially vulnerable to groups who pursue their group interest with a direct and healthy passion.
2) Socialism has caused us, we European peoples, to stand aside while the accomplishments of our ancestors, centuries in the making, are undone, subverted, or forgotten.
3) Socialism leaves us passive in the face of steady changes now occurring with respect to emotional reactions that we European peoples have to the words, names, and stories of our own history. It may seem trivial, for example, that George Washington, once "the father of his country," is now a "slave owner" and a "dead white male." Be well assured, these changes are far from trivial.
4) Socialism leaves us passive as other people occupy our lands. This is a failure in the most basic way that the males of any species can fail. We are letting conditions emerge -- **when such need not be the case** – that will lead to our children being displaced or forced to engage in brutal conflict in order to defend themselves. In addition, socialism leads to our women becoming carriers not of our unique heritage, but rather of a genetic heritage that is not ours. Unless we change the stories that we tell and act upon, we will cease to exist as a unique expression of nature.

Our unwillingness (we men of and from Europe) to define and to defend our interests as a people makes it easy for cohesive groups to bend to their purpose our institutions. Such groups – including now a group made up of our own political leadership -- have turned us into scapegoats, meaning: they blame us for their failures. They do this not because we are white, or because of what we have done to them, or because of anything that our ancestors did, but because **we are passive and do not defend ourselves.**

Another Cost of Socialism: The Flat Society

Consider a man who has state power, a politician let's say (to keep the terminology simple). It is in the interest of this politician to loosen constraints that prevent him from doing what he wants. Constraints that are binding come from men with non-state links to each other. To make this point in the starkest way possible, consider a slave owner. What gives the slave owner power is his ownership of the labor of other men. He has a resource under his control to use not only to curb the power of the politician, but also to maintain close links with other slave owners. How does the politician counter the power of the slave owner? He does so by extending rights to everybody, including the slave. Second Synthesis ideology is the perfect vehicle for this endeavor. In the name of equality, the politician first eliminates obvious affronts to equality, such as the right of one man to own the labor of another man. Next the politician weakens rich men and titled families via taxes, inheritance laws, and violence if necessary. Next, the politician makes gender roles and sexual preferences grist for his mill. In the United States of the present day a man is so hemmed in by the state that he cannot decide who he wants to hire to work for him or choose the kind of people that he would prefer to have living around him in his neighborhood. He cannot even open a bar for the specific, stated, advertised purpose of providing a place where people can sit indoors out of the elements, have a drink, talk to each other, and smoke cigarettes at the same time.

The politician's ideal social order is one in which NO links exist between individuals except for the links that he controls via his control of the state. The landscape that reflects the politician's ideal is a flat plain extending out in all directions, in the middle of which stands a single, tall mountain, the state, at the top of which he sits.

The Flat Society and Its Consequences

Let us for a moment think about Thomas Jefferson in 18th century Virginia. He enjoyed a position of high standing, which he did not have to fight to attain. Social capital (narratives, habits, customs, laws, usages) guided him into the role of slave owner. The same inheritance of social capital guided other men into the role of slave. The existence of this social capital freed Mr. Jefferson from having to devote his energies to the task of beating other men into submission, one outcome of which was that he had the time and leisure to reflect, to explore topics of interest, to study political history, to play a key role in the construction of a new nation, to be the president of the new nation, to build Monticello, to found the University of Virginia, and much else (including a twenty year record of the temperature of water in a spring near Monticello). Call Mr. Jefferson's values "liberal," and describe them with words like "science," "learning," and "careers open to talent." The men who believed in these liberal values considered a society that tolerated the institution of slavery to be flawed. Such men, including Mr. Jefferson himself, saw liberal values as providing a guide to use to reform flawed institutions inherited from the past, including the institution of slavery.

Fine.

Now perform a thought experiment. Suppose that all social capital in 18th century Virginia disappeared. If a man in this suddenly transformed Virginia wanted a slave, he would have to do the dirty work himself of beating another man into submission. Thinking along these lines leads to a question: what role did social capital actually play in Thomas Jefferson's Virginia? The answer is that it established super-ordinate and subordinate categories of men and women, then conveyed these categories across the generations in such a way that brutal battles to establish stratification did not have to be re-fought in each generation.

At the heart of European civilization were generations of men like Thomas Jefferson. Not many had his great curiosity and his graceful style of expression, but many had what he had and more in the way of estates, books, correspondence, discipline, high intellect, and dense social networks. They also had an inheritance of social capital that channeled them into a position of high degree and their servants into positions of low degree. It was not always thus. The origin of European civilization did not start out in a sheltered place. But European peoples established their hierarchies so firmly that it was possible for those at the top to enjoy sufficient leisure and tranquility to create by talent and by patronage an inventory of public goods of great value, e.g., delicate manners, beautiful architecture, a profound literature, mathematics, science, and an artistic tradition of beauty, depth and scope. At the level of day-to-day domestic life, force did not disappear from the world created by European peoples, but it receded. Those with high social altitude lived in a sheltered space that they were able to pass along to the next generation. Violence occurred in this world initially to establish hierarchies and always to chastise the rebellious, but violence mainly existed in the form of matters among men having to do with questions of honor and with neo-feudal clashes of state against state. These neo-feudal clashes tended to be like boulders falling into a creek. After the upheaval caused by a boulder hitting the water, the current of life would resume flowing along about the same as always.

Then came two mutually reinforcing tsunamis: the Second Synthesis and the Industrial Revolution. Under the influence of these two waves, ideas developed in the protected space at the top of the social order spread downward to lower gradations of the collective. The effect was pronounced. The stable hierarchies of Europe came to be seen *not* as bastions of order, taste, manners, beauty, and continuity, but as impediments to progress and barriers to equality. The result was the arrival on the scene of the above-mentioned thought experiment (disappearance of social capital establishing rank) -- only it was not a thought experiment. It actually happened. The social capital that sorted men into super-ordinate and subordinate positions lost vitality.

In the new order that emerged, people embraced the liberal aspects of Mr. Jefferson's vision. However, people did not embrace the non-liberal aspects of Mr. Jefferson's inheritance, i.e., the social capital that channeled him into a position of high degree and his servants into positions of low degree. People were confident that liberal values (such as equality) could be applied universally. Their confidence was misplaced. This did not happen. The two aspects of Mr. Jefferson's world – a legacy of social capital establishing rank peacefully *AND* liberal values -- turned out to be linked. Once the legacy of social capital that established rank peacefully lost vitality, what followed was not Mr. Jefferson's liberal vision of society minus slavery. Rather, what followed was a raw fight for political power.

The Rise of the Psychopath

A flat society is a level plain with a single high mountain, the state. To gain power it is necessary to climb that mountain. The problem with a flat society is that there are no men sitting at the top of their own *monticelli* – their own little mountains – with the education, resources, confidence, networks, and discipline required to stop, filter out, or derail psychopaths, i.e., men of no scruples and of no remorse. Once those who formed an established strata at the top of the social order lost confidence and vitality, there were no men around who were strong enough, linked enough, educated enough, attentive enough, confident enough, or brave enough to stop psychopaths from reaching the top of the mountain and capturing the state.

And indeed, this happened. Psychopathic politicians, bureaucrats, Zionists, and crony capitalists captured the American Republic, not long after which they created a nucleus of crime at the center of the American government. Next, they spread their criminality overseas, in the process of which they kicked it up a notch -- indeed, up many notches. *Coups,* intimidation, murder, false-flag events (e.g., operation Gladio), and ginned up war became standard operating procedure. The tactics and strategies that these men put into practice oversea were soon brought home.

Where we stand now is not edifying to contemplate. Formal democratic process has been reduced to devitalized ritual and incantation. The real politics of Washington take place out of sight among cabals, micro-sovereign groups, plutocrats, aliens, foreigners, and false flag impresarios. Edmund Burke saw it all a long time ago.

> ... criminal means once tolerated are soon preferred. ... Justifying perfidy and murder for public benefit ... public benefit soon becomes the pretext, and perfidy and murder the end. [18]

The government entity located in the city of Washington is now not so much a government as it is this: a vast criminal enterprise.

---

[18] Burke, Edmund. ***Reflections on the Revolution in France***, Penguin books, p.138.

Essay Three

The Idea of Men

Why does Mother Nature make Her large, multi-cellular creatures come in two versions, male and female? The answer is genetics, you say, and you are right. Genetics is one reason, but surely Mother Nature -- i.e., evolution, i.e., life -- could have found a more efficient way to handle the mechanics of creating individual variation while at the same time transmitting information to a next iteration of itself. It seems a bit inefficient, don't you think, that one half of Her large creatures – we males – are unable to reproduce? There must be a reason for this. As it turns out, there is. Said reason is attraction. Call it love if you want. Now think about the following question: where does this powerful, love-driven process occur? On the surface of planet earth -- is the answer -- within a band less than five miles high. This tiny band where life takes place is why there are two sexes. Each has a role to play: that of the female is reproduction, while that of the male is to deal with the consequence of reproduction, which consequence, if unchecked, would soon lead to our extinguishing ourselves like yeast in a Petri dish. The job of the male of the species is to create space by confronting other males, by keeping them at bay, by showing them that our "us" is stronger than their "them," by killing them if necessary. This is what men do. This is why we are here. Now consider a crucial third question: what happens if we men stop doing our job? To answer this question, I am going to re-tell the story of our sojourn on planet earth, but this time from the point of view of the male of the species (and inevitably, too, from the point of view of Western Europe and North America, not because I am arrogant and Euro-centric, but because I am humble and do not presume to speak about the history of other peoples).

(European) Men through the Ages

For most of our existence as a species we men hunted game, tried to best other men in the mating game, and protected our territory from "them," i.e., from other members of our species. Meanwhile women gathered plants, prepared food, tried to mate with the most vital of the men around them, gave birth to babies, tended to the kids, etc.

Due to the pressure of numbers and due also to our cleverness as a species we human creatures made an almost instant transition to agriculture. Women very likely played a major role in this process. We men, however, did not tarry. We quickly jumped on the bandwagon of agriculture and began claiming territories and establishing hierarchies.

Agriculture was so successful that within four or five hundred generations we human creatures found ourselves once again bumping against the sides of our Petri dish. This led to industrialization, a transition carried out by men.

When industrialization arose among those of us living in Western Europe and North America, Christianity was the dominant narrative. Six, seven, or eight generations later the dominant narrative had become Second Synthesis OUGHT TO BE stories taken from the contractarian school of thought. We men were the driving force of this change.

Contract doctrine proved to be a huge success at first. It led to men who thought like scientists and philosophers, while they yet retained the morals and sensibilities of their Christian heritage. These men created wealth in the economy and in the political arena they created a decent approximation of the rule of law, both significant accomplishments, but achieved at a cost.

In the past boys were expected to defend themselves with their fists, and men were expected to defend their honor via a duel if necessary. Classify these expectations and responses under the heading of "male culture." This culture required of a man that he establish a reputation such that if you trenched upon him you could expect to trigger in him a strong response.[19]

With the rise of the rule of law among European peoples, life became easier for men. Violence was taken over and monopolized by the state. A man's reputation based on his willingness to respond fiercely if trenched upon was no longer crucial to his maintaining his position in the community. The role of men as men – men *qua* men – was institutionalized via the creation of a police force. This had consequences. Male culture, upon being taken over by the state, was bureaucratized, the outcome of which was that men became less touchy about honor and more concerned with matters having to do with perks, salaries, and status based on money. Male culture lost vitality to the point of almost vanishing from sight. Manipulation, not valor, become the most useful skill.

Meanwhile, however, on the other hand, history did not stop. It kept rolling along. The success of contract doctrine was followed within a handful of generations by the failure of contract doctrine. The contractarian time bomb went off, the social order fragmented, and communities made up of European peoples became post Babel. Then guess what happened? Men reappeared on stage, though not very attractive men to be sure. Psychopaths, *mafiosi*, *narco-traficantes*, Neo-cons, deep state Machiavellians, gangsters, billionaire *idiot savants* -- such were the type-men who began acquiring power in the political arena. Though crude and

[19] The character, Hotspur, is a classic expression of male culture. He says about bargaining where honor is at stake that he will "cavil on the ninth part of a hair." Shakespeare, *Henry IV, part II*, line 1684

morally ugly, nevertheless, even so, **they were men**. Power was what they wanted. To kill to get power was a step that they were willing to take. They smelled weakness and their noses were good. There *was* weakness.

These unattractive but real men began trenching upon us. What happened? Nothing! They pushed and we did not push back. We, the Best, had not been tempered by the rigors of a vital male culture. We had not taken the measure of each other or of ourselves. We did not know who among us was brave, or would be a good leader, or a worthy lieutenant, or who among us was dishonorable and untrustworthy. We had no families who by tradition provided leadership. (The Kennedy family was tending in this direction until its alpha males were killed off.) We, the so-designated Best, were not ready physically, morally, socially, or spiritually to deal with stage-one men. The poets as usual picked up vibes early on:

> I am not a prophet — and here's no great matter;
> I have seen the moment of my greatness flicker,
> And I have seen the eternal Footman hold my coat,
>   and snicker,
> And in short, I was afraid[20]

What can be done?

The answer to this question starts where it always does, with story. We need a new one. What we do not need, however, is yet another version of the same old contractarian narrative that we have been telling each other for three hundred years. The time has arrived to explore with more flexibility the interaction of story, emotion, and circumstance that is human life on planet earth.

---

[20] TS Eliot *The Love Song of J Alfred Prufrock*

Three Dramas

(Dialogues in voices)

I am now going to tell three stories, one about monarchy and aristocracy, one about our most formidable opponent, the Jews, and one about divinity, but first I want to offer three quotes from Ortega y Gasset and one from Flannery O'Connor.

Ortega has been a source of insight from beginning to end on my intellectual journey, perhaps because he was writing at a time when his country was grinding towards a major conflagration, the Spanish civil war. We people of and from Europe are in a similar place. In our various countries, in our various ways we are grinding towards something that does not bode well.

First quote from Ortega: ".... shipwreck is the truth of life... for which reason I believe only in the thoughts of shipwrecked men."[21] By shipwreck he meant to be pitched into a medium that was inhospitable, and to be forced to exert oneself to stay afloat. Were he alive today he would be interested in us. If ever there were a group of shipwrecked men, flailing about in the water and clinging to pieces of debris, it is us, we men of and from Europe.

Second quote from Ortega: "In order for philosophy to rule, it is not necessary that philosophers become rulers... [or] that rulers philosophize.... it is only necessary that there IS philosophy."[22] I agree with this comment but would like to build a foundation under it. In order for there to be philosophy, there has to be thinking. In order for there to be thinking there has to be discourse. In order for discourse to be useful it has to occur in a forum in which truth

---

[21] Ortega y Gasset, José. Obras Completas, tomo IV, p. 397-398

[22] Ortega Y Gasset, José. Op cit. La rebelión de las masas, p.146, footnote.

is the highest court of appeal (i.e., where it matters whether or not something is true, and where the effort to determine whether or not something is true is a legitimate form of discourse). In order for truth to be the highest court of appeal, laws protecting freedom of speech are helpful. However, do not kid yourself, more than law is needed. Truth requires courage. Where there are no men of courage, there is going to be no forum in which truth is the highest court of appeal. Ah, but where do men of courage come from? Not from logic, not from the logos, not from reason, but from narratives, hierarchies, and circumstances that create pride, confidence, and *esprit de corps*.

The third quote from Ortega I have already cited and you have already read if you read the introduction to this book. It is the quote in which Ortega describes two types of European men, one Germanic, the other Mediterranean. I call attention to this quote for reasons that are personal. The fragmentation of our communities applies to me and makes me Mediterranean, but with this difference: I am a man with Mediterranean sensibilities who aspires to reach the Germanic goal of locating myself in the universe.

The three stories that I am going to tell are not essays. Rather, they are dialogues, that is, plays or dramas with two characters. The speech of one is in italics; the speech of the other is not. I do not claim that this is the best way to proceed, but rather, that it is an attempt to make a virtue out of a necessity. Dialogue makes it possible for a man who lacks internal cohesion -- yet nevertheless who aspires to reach the Germanic goal of figuring out where he stands in relation to the universe -- to tell stories in which different points of view are explicit. Essays, on the other hand, require a unified point of view, which in my case would mean having at the beginning what I aspire to get closer to by the time I reach the end.

This leads to the Flannery O'Connor quote, found in the book *Mystery and Manners*. I identify with it even though I well understand that the quality of her reading material is higher than is the quality of mine. The quote is as follows: "I do not know what I think until I read what I have written."

DRAMA NUMBERONE

THE THIRD QUEEN

(a dialogue in voices)

I am now going to tell a different story.

About what?

A stratified social order headed by a king.

You have to be joking. How can such a story be anything but a stunt to gain attention?

Hear me out then decide for yourself.

To establish one man with the authority of a king is playing with fire, don't you think?

At this time in our history, we are in a war for dominance. The war is not a war of all against all. Rather, for now, the war is against us, we European peoples, in which we are at a huge disadvantage. Our own leaders do not want us to achieve ethnic solidarity and apparently do not care about our survival as a people. Their betrayal makes us vulnerable. We do not have leaders whose interests align with ours such that their fighting for their interests advances ours. On the other hand, our opponents have sources of violence that they can direct against us. The Washington deep state has CIA assassins; Zionists have Mossad hit men; mafia gangs and drug cartels have paid killers; and black people have mobs willing to riot at the drop of a hat. As for us, we people of and from Europe, we have no way to defend ourselves except via an increasingly compromised legal system. At the very least we have to have a street presence of some sort that fights for us, however crudely.

You sound like a European fascist of the 1930s. This is dangerous territory. Do you really want black-shirted gangs rampaging in the streets, intimidating people?

I know what I say sounds evil to white people of relentless goodwill, but goodwill un-backed by menace counts for little in this or in any other age. Besides, relentless goodwill is suspect, don't you think? Is it not a way to hide from ourselves a lack of valor?

What are you saying?

We have to have a way to act in concert to protect ourselves. Given the chaos and disintegration of the present age, this means that we have to have a stage one organization with a leader whose interests align with ours, however crudely. This could take many forms, some quite unsavory. The best model of stage one leadership is a king embedded in a class structure. Yes, I know, this sounds crazy to people of the present age, but don't accuse me of playing with fire. Flames are raging. Unless we learn to play with fire, our world is soon going to be burnt to the ground.

But kings and queens! Why are you talking like this?

Let me begin my answer to your question in an unexpected place. An essay written by William Barrett, which appeared in *Commentary* more than forty years ago, was about tensions between

Lionel Trilling on one side and Delmore Schwarz -- and behind Delmore Schwarz, Philip Rahv -- on the other. Trilling was a well-known liberal writer of the 1940s and 1950s. Rahv was the editor of *Partisan Review*, a magazine to which Trilling contributed. The source of the tension between these men was a difference of opinion about communist literature ("socialist realism"), which Trilling said was "dull, bathetic, stereotyped, and shallow compared to the literature of earlier ages that made use of class distinctions... that portrayed characters who within their class and station... seemed able to develop a rich personality...."[23]

Lionel Trilling's defense of the superior literature of the past had dangerous implications for the Marxists of *Partisan Review*. As William Barrett put it, the danger was that Trilling:

> ".... might seduce us to think the unthinkable thought ... that the conditions which led to a more interesting literature also produced a more satisfying life within society itself. If in the literature of the past we observe human personality developing its varied riches within the framework of class distinctions, might it not be that those distinctions permitted, and in their own way even promoted, the well-being of society?"[24]

The thought that a superior literature might be an indication of a superior society was not shocking to me. I found it easy to believe that a class society not only produced better art but a better person. However, I did not let myself spin out the implications of this thought. The water I swam in -- contract doctrine -- was too close to be able to be aware of its influence. Monarchy, in so far as I thought about it, was an anachronism (or in England, a tourist

[23] Barrett, William, *Commentary*, Feb. 1982 p.40

[24] Ibid. p.40

attraction). Not until I grasped just how *present* to us is our hunting-and-gathering *past* was I able to put contractarian ideas into a proper framework -- and not until putting contractarian ideas in a proper framework was I able to see monarchy as an alternative, indeed, in the long run, for us, we people of and from Europe, as perhaps the only viable alternative.

What makes monarchy healthier than democracy?

The first argument for monarchy, as William Barrett hints, is that it leads to a better literature (and to better art in general, which is not trivial). As a second argument for monarchy, consider a point that is important – indeed crucial – but nevertheless abstract and hard to connect to human passion. The political arena is a commons, by which I mean, a space open to all. What a king does is privatize this space, the outcome of which is that he has an incentive to maintain the health and vitality of an asset that is, in effect, his property. This avoids a tragedy of the commons.

A tragedy of the commons? [25]

Suppose that ten families own a pasture in common, on which each family has the right to graze their own (privately owned) cattle. Suppose that the carrying capacity of the pasture is ten cows. If each family puts out one cow, the outcome is stable. The productivity of the pasture is not degraded. However, should one family set out a second cow, bringing the total number of cows on the pasture to eleven, the carrying capacity of the pasture is exceeded, causing it to deteriorate. The deterioration caused by the

[25] See essay by Garrett Hardin, "The Tragedy of the Commons." https://www.garretthardinsociety.org/articles/art_tragedy_of_the_commons.html

eleventh cow is an expense borne by all ten families. The benefits of the eleventh cow, however, accrue to the one family who owns it. If the other families do nothing, the pasture slowly degrades. To capture at least some benefit before the pasture is ruined, the other families have to put out additional cows, which accelerates the pasture's destruction. This is the tragedy of the commons.

What is the solution to the problem of the commons?

Libertarians say that the solution is to give to each family one tenth of the pasture as private property. If a family then overgrazes its parcel, it gets all the benefit but also bears all of the cost. The problem with the libertarian solution is that it is not a solution. What happens is that the problem of the commons is shifted from one place, the pasture, to a different place, the forum where decisions about the pasture are made.

By way of contrast the classical socialist wants to nationalize the pasture then manage it by a government agency for the benefit of "society." This also is a non-solution. It is, in fact, the same non-solution as that of the libertarians. Both depend on activity in the political arena. Neither understands that the political arena itself is a commons vulnerable to all the counterproductive feedback loops inherent in that form of ownership. Monarchy offers the possibility of establishing a political structure that dampens down the tendency for negative feedback loops to emerge.

A third argument for monarchy is this: each individual has to accommodate his emotional reactions to the authority of the king and to the gradations of the social order that the king establishes and backs up. The result is a community of individuals whose emotional reactions tend to become complementary as they conform to the power and interests of the hierarchy. This is what Lionel Trilling caught a glimpse of, to wit: that lives are richer when lived under the discipline of a class structure. Nicolas Gomez-Davila makes a somewhat similar point with aphorism number 764.

> "In societies where everybody believes they are equal, the inevitable superiority of a few makes the rest feel like failures. Inversely, in societies where inequality is the norm, each person settles into his own distinct place, without feeling the urge to compare himself to others. Only a hierarchical structure is compassionate towards the mediocre and the meek."[26]

Democracy, by way of contrast, maps into each individual a series of narrative strands in which no single strand has the vitality to impose itself across the width and breadth of the community. Each narrative strand develops its own community with its own definitions of high-and-low and them-and-us. Among these fragmented groups is to be found the psychopath and his gang. Nothing stops the most competent and ruthless of these gangs from capturing the sovereignty of the state. What the institution of monarchy does is confer a special status upon one such gang, the outcome of which is that the man who becomes the monarch has an incentive to suppress other psychopaths in the system. He also has a reason to care about the future wellbeing of his sovereign unit, which is his property and will in time become the property of a son or daughter. An unintended consequence of monarchy is that the sensibilities and manners of the population, in their various stations in life, tend to become complementary, thereby giving structure, continuity, and coherence to the kingdom.

---

[26] Nicolas Gomez-Davila: Translated by "Stephen." https://don-colacho.blogspot.com/2011/03/2943.htm

Monarchy is not intellectually an ideal form of government but look at the results. A thousand years of monarchy put us, we European peoples, at the pinnacle of human vitality and creativity. By way of comparison, it has taken only seven, eight, or nine generations of belief in contractarian stories for us to render ourselves certifiable for commitment to an insane asylum. We squabble over absurdities – can a man turn himself into a woman or vice-versa – while remaining passive as our homelands are colonized by foreigners.

What is all too evident is that you do not believe in the republic that you grew up in, the United States of America?

The Founding Fathers of the republic that I grew up in made heroic efforts to carry out a project towards the accomplishment of which they brought a rare combination of integrity, knowledge of history, and capacity to act. In spite of their courage, competence, and wisdom, however, they failed. Why -- you might ask -- given that they were not naïve and knew full well that governments attract unscrupulous men? Their mistake was to overestimate the effectiveness of institutional design (separation of powers, judges with life tenure, duties carefully assigned to the various branches of government, et cetera), while at the same time they underestimated the importance of Cross and Crown in the formation of sensibility.

What prevents the king from being a tyrant?

Words written on a piece of paper and called by a special name – a constitution -- do not restrain the man who controls the violence of the state. Such a man is held within the bounds of law by other men. Laws are necessary, to be sure. However, when dealing with sovereign power, laws are lines in the sand. When a transgression of law occurs, a subsequent event also has to occur: to wit: men have to be prepared to swing into the saddle and ride hard. If none do so, there is going to be no rule of law. To rely on institutional design is to rely on a fairytale.

That's strong language.

Let me give some examples. George C. Patton died in 1945, under strange circumstances one week before he was to return to Washington, where he planned to oppose many powerful interests. James Forrestal, Truman's first Secretary of Defense, was a man of great perspicacity. In the late 1940s, when lines of power in post-World War II Washington were being established, he wanted to make public the black budget of the OSS (Office of Special Services, which became the CIA). He also wanted no recognition of the State of Israel. His ideas were opposed by powerful and dangerous men. What happened to him is not pretty to contemplate. Declared to be mentally ill, held at the Naval Hospital in Bethesda, Maryland, reported to have committed suicide by leaping out of a window on the 16th floor – **that** was what happened to him, almost certainly a case of murder staged as suicide.[27]

In the case of both Patton and Forrestal lines were transgressed, that is to say, laws were broken. Dealing with these transgressions required that men **first and foremost let themselves see what happened,** then swing into action. Too few did so to make a difference. The killers of Patton and Forrestal successfully used violence to establish political outcomes of crucial importance with respect to the distribution of power in post-World War II Washington. If you think I exaggerate, meditate on this: since the late 1940s,

---

[27] See David Martin, *The Assassination of James Forrestal,* Second edition, McCabe Publishing, Hyattsville, Maryland. 2021

when these issues were sorted out, how much damage has the CIA done and how much damage has Israel done? The answer is straightforward. The men who had the power to impose Israel upon us and the men who captured and ran the CIA (as it has been run these seventy years) destroyed the American republic.

To give another example of a moment when men were required but not present, consider the case of William Colby, former head of the CIA, who one day disappeared, only to show up a week later as a corpse washed ashore in Chesapeake Bay. Very likely he was the victim of CIA machinations. Were the local authorities – prosecutors, sheriffs, district attorneys, etc. – courageous enough to pursue this case, they might have exposed sordid truths about the CIA, but courage these local authorities did not have and the truth about Colby remained undiscovered. The men who murdered him increased the power and fear of the criminal gang (operating inside the state but outside the law) known as the CIA. The power of this gang was enhanced by being unchallenged and -- even more damaging -- by being unspoken.

When the affairs of ordinary citizens are at stake, institutional design works. Legislators, district attorneys, judges, juries, *et al* do their job and the system functions as well or as poorly as can be expected of human institutions. But when George Patton suffers a strange accident, when James Forrestal falls out of a window from the 16th floor, when William Colby disappears from view -- to wash ashore a week later -- it can reasonably be inferred that foul play is involved and that important issues are at stake. It is at these moments that men have to swing into the saddle and ride hard. None did so in post-World War II Washington. Patton was successfully "accidented," Forrestal was successfully defenestrated, Colby (a generation later) was successfully drowned, constraints on the illegitimate use of power in Washington were successfully mocked, and deeply harmful policies were successfully implemented. A failure across the board of such magnitude, uncorrected after three generations, is not a micro failure of individuals but a macro failure of the model. **The type-men who must be present to make democracy work are not produced in a democracy.**

I think you exaggerate, but even if democracy leads to pusillanimity, what is the alternative?

Tell a different story. Maybe the best story we could tell would be about a return to what we are, a hunting-and-gathering species, but this is not going to happen unless we do such violence to ourselves that only a few survive. In my opinion, the story that has a chance of leading to a long-term, viable solution for us, we European people, is neo-monarchy. What happens in a neo-monarchy is that we find ways to recapitulate self-consciously the journey from hunting-and-gathering to civil society that our ancestors made unselfconsciously.

I don't understand what you just said. What makes a monarchy "neo?"

In the 17th,18th, and 19th centuries the transition made by European peoples from monarchy to contractarian government was fairly quick, considering that a major restructuring occurred with respect to how men acquire and deploy sovereign power (i.e., how men kill other men with impunity). For a few generations, as I have said time and again, the transition gave us the best of both worlds: the flexibility of new ideas together with the morals, the discipline, and the social coherence of our Christian heritage. But, as I have also said many times, contract doctrine does not work. It takes us on a journey that starts with order but ends with disorder. By way of contrast, the journey that historical monarchies took our ancestors on started with disorder but ended in a condition of order. The order that emerged was unintended. My understanding of neo-monarchy turns on this point. The order that was an unintended consequence of historical monarchies becomes an intended consequence of neo-monarchies. The *raison d'être* of a neo-monarchy, I am saying, is to locate ourselves within hierarchical structures such that over time sensibilities emerge that lead to relationships among individuals, families, and groups that are complementary.

You are delusional if you think that a monarchy embedded in a class structure can be resurrected. We can get ourselves a dictator easily enough, but a monarchy embedded in a class structure -- that's a different matter altogether. No real alternative exists except to make some kind of liberal democratic arrangement work. Ortega y Gasset was right about that.

Part of what you just said I agree with. The disarray of our sensibilities in the present age makes authoritarian government inevitable. The issue at stake for us now is who is going to achieve dominance. The situation we are living through is discouraging. The men with power in our own governments want to break our spirit.

Why do they want to break our spirit?

...to achieve dominance over us in the realm of sensibility....

What can we do about it?

....impose tough training regimens upon ourselves....

What do you mean?

We are not going to extricate ourselves from our present difficulties by coming up with the right law, or the right distribution of assets, or the right technology. What first has to happen is that we European males turn ourselves back into men and start doing a man's job. To impose discipline upon ourselves is the first step that has to be taken for any project of recovery to be successful.

You are just saying words. This is mumbo jumbo.

I don't think so. We are not helpless. Two crucial dimensions of life exist where we can make a difference, one is small and real, and the other is big and abstract. The small, real dimension is a single life: mine, yours, his. The big, abstract dimension is a map of the circumstance. With respect to the small dimension, we individual men have a lot of control. We can impose discipline upon ourselves. With respect to the big, abstract dimension – i.e., the map we use to navigate through life -- we also have control. We can modify or discard our current map by telling a different story. Most of life involves the interaction of the micro (a life) with the macro (stories told to orient us as we play the game of life).

I still don't understand the point that you are making.

We can live with discipline (or not) and we can modify or change the story that we tell to guide ourselves through the circumstance (or not). With discipline and a good story, we win at every stage provided we keep in mind that winning means living a life of meaning and purpose.

Here is a simple model of what I am saying:

Strong individual discipline + a good story = win the game of life.

Strong individual discipline + a bad story = lose the game of life.

Strong individual discipline + use of the habit of discipline to tell a better story = win the game of life.

No discipline + the best story ever devised = lose the game of life.

No discipline + just about the worst story that you can imagine = where we are now. (Given where we are now, how can we fail to improve ourselves, even if what we accomplish amounts to nothing more than a Francis Macomber moment?)

You think that contract doctrine is a bad story.

Yes.

You want to change it?

Yes.

You think that monarchy is a better story?

I think that neo-monarchy is a better story.

How do we establish a neo-monarchy?

Start by telling stories about it. *The Communist Manifesto* came out in 1848. By 1917 the communists had themselves a state.

What does your so-called neo-monarchy look like?

Consider three points. Think of these points as a model, i.e., as a simple story about a complex story. (The third point, in fact, contains a model within the model).

1) A neo-monarchy is not one monarch but a patchwork of monarchies, each in a region and each embedded in a class structure consisting of a king, an aristocracy, and commoners. Each kingdom is an ethno-state. The principal job of the king is to protect his sovereign unit from other sovereign units. Each kingdom has to

be small enough so that the upper strata do not lose sight of their dependency on the lower strata. When a sovereign unit becomes big or diverse -- and especially when it becomes big and diverse -- it becomes easy to be captured by a small, cohesive class, group, gang, or tribe. I do not think that there is any solution to the problem of capture except size. A small sovereign unit is harder to capture than a large one for a simple reason: information in the small unit -- about who is doing what to whom -- is more accessible. Also, small sovereign units are more likely to have populations that are homogeneous, thereby making it easier to do what is always hard to do, make the purpose of government not the health of government, but the health of the population.

2) Aristocracy is the most important layer in the various gradations of the social order. It is where the contradictions of civilized life are reconciled. For there to be what we call "civilization," toughness and authority have to be established and, at the same time, they have to be reconciled with discipline, good taste, candid discourse, and self-restraint. Shakespeare as usual sees deeply into these matters.

> They that have power to hurt and will do none,
> That do not do the thing they most do show,
> Who, moving others, are themselves as stone,
> Unmoved, cold, and to temptation slow:
> They rightly do inherit heaven's graces
> And husband nature's riches from expense;[28]

How brilliant and deep is the line "husband nature's riches from expense!" This is what healthy men do: i.e., prevent nature from being used up (at the risk of their own lives when necessary). This sonnet also contains an admonition. Strong men when they go bad, they go really bad. "Lilies that fester smell far worse than weeds."

---

[28] Shakespeare, William. Sonnet number 90

Aristocrats, to be able to reconcile opposites, have to have the confidence that comes from occupying a position of high social standing and also that comes from having access to resources. Although it could seriously backfire, and thus be a bad idea, I would at least look into the possibility of re-establishing the old *code duelist* in some form or manner.

You cannot be serious! You want aristocrats to be touchy, arrogant, privileged, and go around shooting each other over affairs of honor?

I want them to live under the discipline of narratives and traditions that weed out phonies and cowards and that induce the noble among them to carry out a crucial task: facilitate the production of public goods (and actions that can be thought of as public goods), such as, for example, constrain the sovereign, support the gradations of the social order, establish forums of discourse in which truth is the highest court of appeal, establish the gradations of the social order in the next generation, provide leadership for the king's cause, and create and patronize high art and high intellect. The individuals who facilitate the production of public goods receive compensation for their efforts not as individuals, but only as members of a group. The job of the aristocracy is to be a group that facilitates the production of public goods. This is what it gets paid to do (as a group). If some men among the aristocracy do not attend to the job of producing public goods, such goods will not be produced. An elite that does not facilitate the production of public good is not an aristocracy, but a criminal gang with state power (which is what we have now).

According to Robert Frost "the only way out is through." This may be true for us now in the short run. However, in the long run, the only way out is *up*. This is because the direction of influence goes from high to low. The discipline and virtue of men of high rank can overcome the corruption and the laziness of men of low rank. It does not work the other way around, however. The discipline and virtue of the low cannot overcome the corruption and decadence of the high.

3) A crucial job of neo-monarchy is to create high art, "the best that has been thought and said"[29] (and pictured, too, I would add). This task applies across the board. Those with genius produce high art no matter where they are located in the social order. Those with money and power buy it, support it as patrons, and let their taste and sensibilities be formed by it over the generations. High art is where neo-monarchy earns its keep. The well-known phrase *de gustibus non disputandum est (*there is no disputing taste) is dead wrong. Taste and sensibility are precisely the issues in dispute. Their transmission across the generations IS civilization. To model point number three, imagine a queen who becomes the third queen of European culture and philosophy.

A third queen??

Yes, she follows the austere Queen Theologica of the first synthesis and the graceless Queen Economica of the second. The authority of this third queen rests not upon theology, not upon economics, not even upon justice, but upon beauty.

You better define what you mean by beauty.

"Wordsworth would have preferred the interpretation of Kant, which he probably heard from Coleridge: that in our experience of the sublime and beautiful in nature, the unknown depths of

---

[29] Arnold, Mathew. *Culture and Anarchy*, (Oxford, Project Gutenberg, 1869) p.7

the self is seen to respond to some unknown and supersensible depths of nature..., and be at one with the latter."[30]

Kant got this one right, or in any case was heading in the right direction. I would simplify his definition, however, in one crucial way. Instead of saying "our experience of the sublime and beautiful in nature," I would say: "all beauty." The definition would then be as follows: all beauty is the unknowable depth of the self in sync with the unknowable depth of nature.

You are going to have a hard time getting people to discard the idea of justice, not to mention the new, only 2500-year-old idea called "democracy," and instead turn to the idea of beauty.

I agree. The modern age sees democracy as a stable political structure that can be built like a house then lived in. The assessment of (some) Greeks was more accurate. They saw democracy as one stop among many on a journey that included aristocracy (rule of the best), plutocracy (the rule of money), monarchy (the rule of one), et cetera.

As for what you say about justice, you are right about that, too. The thought of a government not even pretending to be based on justice would cause feelings of panic in the population. Even so the concept is thin. Stories about justice come in one of two versions. If I have something that you want, justice means that I do **not** have to give you any. Or, on the other hand, if you have something that I want, justice means that you **do** have to give me some. The action that results from stories about justice is a politics of deception.

---

[30] Op. cit. *Commentary*, Feb. 1982, p. 44

What is the action that results from the idea of a new queen, a queen of beauty?

A politics of stratification.

You consider stratification to be desirable!

Yes. What starts as a stratification of the social order leads to a stratification of values, which leads to a stratification of sensibility, which leads to the creation of high art, which is a public good of immense benefit to all.

What is so great about high art?

We human creatures -- built to roam -- are now forced to live in a manner that is unnatural. High art gives us the training, discipline, and sensibilities that we have to have to see and appreciate the majesty of life in all of its beauty, but also to see and accept the sternness of life in all of its implacability. Another way to make the same point is to say that high art offers a way to carry out a meta-task, integration of consciousness (of the sort that language makes possible) into the web of life. We are a long way from accomplishing this meta-task.

The idea of a meta-task sounds like the beginning of a discussion about one world government.

No, wrong, the opposite. One world government = slavery. What has to happen is not aggregation but disaggregation. As I have said time and again, the problem with big and/or diverse sovereign units is that they are easy to be captured by a smaller, more cohesive group, tribe, or gang. Even in the case where the population of a big sovereign unit is homogeneous, the people at the top nevertheless have a strong incentive to coalesce into an "us" that exploits (and all too often degrades) those arrayed down below. Size matters. It may well be that of all the variables that support civilized life, the size of the sovereign unit is the most important. Beyond a certain size -- not easy to determine -- sovereignty is toxic.

What is the role of high art in the carrying out of this meta-task?

To repeat myself yet again, the role of high art is to give us the mental tools and the sensibilities that we have to have to deal with the circumstance the way it is, not with the way that we would like for it to be. Consider once again the 18th and 19th centuries. We European peoples, due to our high art and discipline, were able not only to envision a new way to organize government, but then to make a transition to the new vision. We soon ran into a problem, however. The story that we chose to reorganize around – contract doctrine – turned out to be a disaster. Not immediately, but in time contractarian narratives led to the destruction of the gradations of the social order on which our civilization depended. We have now devolved into a post Babel confusion of such stupidity, vulgarity, ugliness, and brutality that our progeny -- if we have any – will be left slack-jawed with stupefaction should they ever be in a position to contemplate what we did with what we had been given.

How do we recover our capacity to create high art?

Discard contract doctrine. Make beauty the court of highest appeal in our forums of discourse. Tell stories about beauty that establishes an order of rank for all the stories that we tell, hence for all the emotions that we feel, hence for all the actions that we take.

I hope you realize just how radical this idea is. You want to put aesthetics over economics and even over justice.

I agree that the idea is radical, but don't complain. I told you that I was going to tell a different story. Nicolas Gomez-Davila nails it with aphorism 2954:

> "What modern man calls "change" is walking ever more rapidly down the same road in the same direction. In this sense, the world has not changed in the last three hundred years. The mere suggestion of true change scandalizes and terrifies modern man...." [31]

Gomez-Davila is right. Change means a different order of rank in our hierarchy of values, a different court of highest appeal in our forums of discourse, and a different understanding of the role of hierarchy in our social order, all of which means that we have to tell a different story and start walking down a different road.

Why do you want beauty to be your highest value?

A flippant (but accurate) answer would be to say:

> Beauty does more than justice can
> To justify God's ways to man.[32]

A more conscientious answer comes out of the definition of beauty ("the unknowable depth of the self in sync with the unknowable depth of nature"). If we want to integrate human consciousness into the web of life, beauty is the road that takes us there. Beauty is the harmonious unity of part and whole, of individual

---

[31] Gomez-Davila Aphorism 2954. Translated by "Stephen," (modified by me). https://don-colacho.blogspot.com/2011/03/2943.htm

[32] The structure of this couplet comes from A E Housman: *Terrence this is stupid stuff,* which itself looks back to John Milton's *Paradise Lost.*

and species, of species and the web of life on the surface of planet earth. Beauty is how we as a species go back to nature. Beauty is the next age of man -- if there is going to be one.

A social order based on the primacy of beauty is a road that nobody will go down.

Don't be so sure. Mother Nature plays a tough game. Beauty is no guarantee of success, but ugliness is a guarantee of failure. Her solutions are beautiful. They have to be. Life on planet earth is mutual interaction. Part and whole have to be in harmony. If we survive, it will be because we go down a road that leads to the creation, preservation, and manifestation of beauty. On the other hand, if we persist in trying to achieve equality and democracy, we will become ever more vulgar and brutal until we go over a cliff, at which time Mother Nature will move on to Her next experiment.

How do we avoid the cliff?

Take a crucial next step.

What step is that?

In the past we rose above the level of being a primate by subordinating ourselves to culture. The crucial next step that now has to be taken is the subordination of our culture to nature.

I have no idea what you are talking about.

The psychopath (or to use my terminology, "the Worst") is unable to express his organizing passions of them-and-us and high-and-low except in a gang that functions at the primate level of emotion and coercion. What changes him from a primate to a man is culture. It does so by making it possible for him to become integrated into complex hierarchies or into the service of a higher vision. As for us (the so-called Best), because we subordinate our lives to our culture, we are not primates. However, even so, we have worked ourselves into a bad place. Our culture has no roots. We have lost touch with the earth. The most basic building blocks of mammalian life – male and female – we blur and conflate. So confused has our relationship with nature become that we face disappearance as a unique creation of nature, or perhaps annihilation by others due to confusion and pusillanimity. The task that we face now is to close the loop.

What does that mean?

Manners are an example of culture. Hierarchy is an example of nature. Our ancestors found ways to subordinate themselves as individuals to culture while at the same time their culture remained subordinate to nature. We now have to figure out how to do self-consciously what they did intuitively.

This is just verbiage. How are you different from the Worst? Behind all of your rhetoric, you want what the psychopath wants, power and dominance.

You are right. However, there is a difference. Psychopaths fight for dominance in a government structure. What this means in practice is that they fight for something small, their own personal power in a state apparatus. We are not fighting for something small. On the contrary, we are fighting for something big: **ourselves as a people living through time in communities and landscapes that are integrated into nature.** Government is a necessary part of our project of recovery -- but a dangerous and tricky part. All governments are vulnerable to being captured by a gang, which gang then bends government to its purpose. For a people to persist through time, the passion that holds them together as a people has to be stronger than the passion that holds a gang together. I will go so far as to say that any sovereign entity **not** integrated into the interests, the history, the usages, the customs, the hierarchies, the passions, and the terrain of a people is an incubator of psychopathology and will soon be captured. Obstacles of every sort stand in way of the health and the continuity of ourselves as a people. Facing and dealing with these obstacles is how the game of life is won (or lost as the case may be)

Drama Number Two

"Them"

What are you going to do now?

Plunge into present day politics in order to address a difficult topic.

About what?

About a group of people who have captured our government.

Who are these people?

Jews, in particular, Zionists.

What are you going to say about them?

We people of and from Europe, on the one hand, and Jews, on the other hand, are two tectonic plates in collision. Historical forces shape our relationship with each other. To simplify the discussion of this relationship, I am going to organize it by asking a question: are the Jews the cause of our problems?

Do you ask this question because you are looking for somebody to blame for your failures or do you blame the Jews because of what they have done to you?

You will have to decide for yourself. My question is a model, that is, a simplification of complexity for the purpose of taking action. I am going to give four answers to the question. My first answer is "no," the Jews are not the cause of our problems. To modify a line from the play *Julius Caesar*: the fault, dear Brutus, lies not in our stars – nor in our Jews – but in ourselves that we are underlings. My second answer to the question, however, is a lengthy and complicated "yes," the Jews **are** the cause of our problems. My third answer is "no" they are not and my fourth answer is "yes," they are.

This doesn't sound coherent to me.

Sorry, it cannot be helped. The story is complicated. My second answer -- which is "yes," the Jews are the cause of our problems -- is organized around the destruction of the Twin Towers in New York City on September 11, 2001, the event now called "9/11." Though far from being the whole story of our relationship with the Jews, 9/11 nevertheless puts in sharp relief the forces at play.

How so?

The evidence that 9/11 was an Israeli operation is overwhelming. However, I am not going to discuss the now all too familiar facts demolishing the official narrative (e.g., WTC 7 in freefall, "pull it," pyroclastic cloud flows spreading over Manhattan, medal in the rubble pile still glowing red hot weeks later, et cetera). In due course I will offer one bit of evidence that has not received the attention that it deserves, a report from the US Geology Survey entitled "Elemental Analysis of Ground Zero." First, however, I want to mention two antecedents to 9/11, the assassination of President Kennedy on November 22, 1963, and the Israeli attack on the USS *Liberty*, on June 8, 1967.

November 22, 1963

The assassination of Kennedy was a *coup d'état* that changed the rules of the game in Washington and brought an end to the American republic. Much effort has gone into trying to identify the perpetrators. Two groups stand out as prime suspects, one domestic, centering around the CIA (Allen Dulles and John Jesus Angleton), and the other foreign. I started off believing that Angleton and/or Allen Dulles were the intellectual authors and organizing force of the assassination. They had a serious difference with Kennedy, which, however, strictly speaking, was not about policy. (Dulles wanted to invade Cuba. Kennedy did not.) My opinion about the tension between the CIA and Kennedy was that it was not about policy *per se*, but about power. Dulles and his men at CIA had carved out a bit of sovereignty for themselves, meaning that they had gathered to themselves the various roles of a sovereign – policemen, prosecutor, judge, jury, and executioner -- one consequence of which was that they were able to kill the occasional man or woman when they deemed it to be necessary.[33] Such power, once tasted by such men, is not easily taken away. Such power Kennedy wanted to take away. **That** was the problem -- I thought -- whether the parties were fully aware of the issue or not.

Although a battle over sovereignty may have figured into the assassination of Kennedy, I now think that my initial view was

---

[33] See Mary's *Mosaic* for a sordid and dishonorable example of the CIA in action.

wrong, or in any case inadequate. Michael Collins Piper, Ron Unz, Laurent Guyenot, and others make a convincing case that the core of the plot to kill Kennedy was a foreign government – Israel -- working in conjunction with native elements, most likely Lyndon Johnson (explicitly or implicitly). Both Johnson and the Israelis had time-sensitive problems with Kennedy. The Israelis wanted the atomic bomb, which Kennedy was preventing them from obtaining. Were Kennedy to have been re-elected in 1964, the Israelis' bomb project would have been delayed by many years. Lyndon Johnson, for his part, due to issues of corruption, was to be dropped from the ticket and might have ended up in jail had Kennedy lived. Both Johnson and the Israelis wanted Kennedy gone and were in a position to do something about it.

June 8, 1967

From the assassination of November 22, 1963, it is possible to draw a line to June 8, 1967, on which day the Israelis assaulted the *USS Liberty* with the intent of killing all the sailors on board and blaming Egypt. They failed. Sailors on the *Liberty* repaired the radio antenna damaged in the initial attack and got out a call for help to an American aircraft carrier. When the commander of the carrier sent planes to investigate, no less a personage than Lyndon Johnson himself, via telephone, ordered that the planes be called back. That Johnson did not want to know what was happening on that fateful day is *prima facie* evidence of complicity. He already knew what was happening. In the aftermath of the assault on the *USS Liberty*, Johnson saw to it that the Israelis were held accountable only for making an error of mistaken identity. As for the Israelis, they acquired significant information as a result of the *Liberty* incident, which was that they could do just about anything they wanted to the Americans and get away with it.

The line that went from the Kennedy assassination to the assault on the *USS Liberty* extended out until it reached the World Trade Center on the morning of September 11, 2001.

9/11

You are saying that the official story is wrong. Not Arabs but the Israelis carried out the assault of 9/11.

The official story is an insult to intelligence, common sense, history, and science.

Most Americans believe that the event was an Arab operation.

9/11 was a psyop that followed the rules of the genre, to wit: establish a narrative ahead of time in forums of public discourse (e.g., *A Clean Break*), yank people out of habitual patterns with an assault, then hit them with phony narratives and planted evidence such as an undamaged passport.

An undamaged passport?

Within a few hours of the collapse of the Twin Towers an intact passport was reported to have been found -- and not just any passport, mind you, but one belonging to one of 19 (supposed) hijackers who (supposedly) commandeered two jets with which they knocked down three very real, very well constructed skyscrapers. That such a sophomoric ploy was not debunked immediately is hard to believe, especially when you consider that no airplane data recorders ever turned up. You have to concede that the perpetrators had a good understanding of us.

What do you mean?

They understood that the event of 9/11 would be so spectacular and the implications so profound that to face the truth would require that a conversion take place.

A conversion?? I'm not following you.

Conversions usually happen after an accumulation of evidence causes an old narrative to lose vitality and a new one to replace it. In the case of 9/11, however, the event was so extraordinary that a conversion has to take place first, as only then can proper weight be given to facts in full view from the beginning. The perpetrators knew this -- or at least sensed it to be the case -- and used it to their advantage by planting lame stories, such as the one about an undamaged passport.

Surely you do not base your indictment of Israel on a story, however implausible, about an undamaged passport.

No, I do not. I will now offer as evidence a report from the United States Geological Survey entitled "An Elemental Analysis of Ground Zero," [34] based on samples collected from around the site. The opening sentence of the report is this:

---

[34] There are curiosities linked to this report. No names are attached and there is no indication about where it was published. If it is a fabrication, whoever wrote it is a talented writer of science fiction. However, a lot suggests that it is not a fabrication. Big sources of energy were in play on the day of 9/11, e.g., the foundation of the Twin Towers were obliterated down to bedrock, not much of a rubble pile was left behind considering that what collapsed were two one-hundred story buildings, medal in the rubble was glowing red hot weeks later, and pyroclastic clouds drifted over Manhattan. How can any of this be accounted for unless there was an enormous release of energy from somewhere?

> "A 2-person USGS crew collected grab samples from 35 localities within a 0.5-1 km radius circle centered on the World Trade Center site on the evenings of September 17 and 18, 2001."

Under the heading of "The Correlation between Barium and Strontium" there is this summarizing paragraph:

> "The USGS took 12 measurements for Barium and Strontium. Using what is called a t test statistic, another statistical technique, we obtain a t value of 21.83 for the correlation coefficient of 0.99 with 12 data points. Without explaining this in detail, what this tells us is that the chance that such a high correlation coefficient could have arisen by chance with 12 measurements is vanishingly small. Nuclear Fission, confirmed."

Under the heading of "conclusions" this is the entirety of what the report says:

> "The graph of Thorium versus Lithium including the Girder Coatings has exactly the same form as the graph showing Thorium versus Uranium, also including the Girder Coatings. Without the two Girder Coatings the correlation of Thorium to Lithium in the dust is completely linear. We therefore have compelling evidence that this fission pathway of Uranium to Thorium and Helium, with subsequent decay of the Helium into Lithium, has indeed taken place. It is out of the question that all of these correlations which are the signature of a nuclear explosion could have occurred by chance. This is impossible. The presence of rare Trace elements such as Cerium, Yttrium and Lanthanum is enough

> to raise eyebrows in themselves, let alone in quantities of 50ppm to well over 100ppm. When the quantities then vary widely from place to place but still correlate with each other according to the relationships expected from nuclear fission, it is beyond ALL doubt that the variations in concentration are due to that same common process of nuclear fission. When we find Barium and Strontium present, in absolutely astronomical concentrations of over 400ppm to over 3000ppm, varying from place to place but varying in lockstep and according to known nuclear relationships – the implications are of the utmost seriousness.
>
> "The presence of Thorium and Uranium correlated to each other by a clear mathematical power relationship – and to other radionucleide daughter products – leaves nothing more to be said. This type of data has probably never been available to the public before. It is an unprecedented insight into the action of a nuclear device. Nuclear weapon scientists around the world will have seized this data to analyze it and try and determine exactly what type of device produced it. September 11th, 2001, was the first Nuclear event within a major United States city and a global financial center of the world and this is the biggest secret of this century, until now."

If a nuclear device were used, why do you blame Israel and the Zionists?

The use of a nuclear bomb means that 9/11 was a government sponsored event. A list of suspect governments is short. Two names are on it: the government entity in Washington and the government entity in Tel Aviv. That elements of both were involved seems likely. However, in my opinion, people in the Israeli government were the intellectual authors and prime perpetrators of the event.

Why do you think that?

Two reasons: *cui bono* and history. Start with history first and go back a long way. The Jews have two sacred books, the *Torah* and the *Talmud.* The *Torah* is the word of God as transcribed from their oral traditions and as revealed by their prophets. The *Talmud,* a compendium of commentaries written by rabbis, is to the *Torah* as scholastic theology is to the Christian understanding of the Bible, i.e., a response to the gift of revelation. A crucial difference exists between the Judaism of the *Torah/Talmud* and Christianity, however, which difference hinges on the promise made by the Hebrew God, Yahweh, to give land to the Hebrew tribes. For the Hebrew Tribes, this land -- this Promised Land -- is a place with a name, Canaan, located on the other side of a river, the Jordan, with people already living there, the Canaanites. The presence of people already living there presents a problem. Where do they fit in? The *Torah's* answer is that they do not fit in. They have to go away. Should they refuse to go away, it is okay to treat them with a different standard of morality. For Christians, by way of contrast, the Promised Land is not a physical place on the other side of an actual river, but a spiritual condition. There is room for the Canaanites in the Promised Land because it is spiritual, not physical. By spiritualizing the idea of the Promised Land, Christians made everybody at least potentially a brother via conversion. Jews, by **not** spiritualizing the idea of the Promised Land, locked themselves into an ironclad ethnocentrism.

The outcome of Jewish ethnocentrism was the emergence of a bifurcated system of morals, with one set for themselves and a different set for non-Jews. This bifurcated system of morals presented a problem to European peoples, but a manageable problem as long as Jews lived apart in *shtetls*. With the rise to dominance of Second Synthesis OUGHT TO BE stories, however, pressure on the Jews abated and they started living among us as ordinary citizens or subjects. Some Jews understood that the same standards of morality had to apply to themselves as to us. Other Jews, however, refused to let go of the bifurcated morality of their sacred books. These unassimilated Jews live among us, too, **but not with us under the discipline of a common moral code.**

Which is a problem?

Yes, a big one. Unassimilated Jews engage in dishonest ethnic networking, lie under oath, defend Jews who they know to be guilty of crime, pursue Zionist goals while presenting themselves as loyal citizens of our country, set up lucrative but shady operations catering to our lowest impulses (gambling, prostitution, pornography, et cetera) and carry out a relentless drumbeat of criticism of us for failing to live up to ideals in which they do not believe, do not follow, have no intention of following, and violate shamelessly in Israel.

Your argument is that Jews have a separate set of morals based on stories from their sacred books. How can this be? Your own model – that stories engender emotion and that emotion issues forth into action -- should cause you to question your understanding of the Jews. They do not believe in Yahweh with the same degree of fervor as did their ancestors, yet nevertheless they work well together as a cohesive, well-defined group. How is it that their archaic stories about Yahweh continue even now to engender in them strong tribal emotion and forceful action?

Good question, which, however, has an answer. The Jews updated the *Torah* with a narrative that does what vital narratives do, to wit: engender strong emotion that issues forth into action. The title of their new, updated narrative is "the Holocaust."

I am not following you.

In the *Torah* Yahweh says to the Hebrew tribes: I am your God. I choose you as my people; I give to you the land of Canaan; and I give you permission to expel or destroy the people who are living there now. [35] About this narrative, what does it do? The answer is that it defines the Hebrew people as special (chosen by Yahweh) and it gives to the Hebrew tribes the right to treat non-Hebrew people by a different standard of morality. Now ask a second question: what does the Holocaust narrative do? Answer: the same thing. It defines Jews as special (a people uniquely singled out by anti-Semites to be eliminated) and under the rubric of "never again" it gives Jews permission to treat non-Jews by a different standard of morality.

The replacement of the Yahweh narrative with the Holocaust narrative explains a curiosity about the Jews. They resent people who also claim to be victims of genocide (such as the Armenians). To defend the uniqueness of their victimization, the Jews resort to every known strategy of law, rhetoric, political manipulation, and discourse **except one.** This one exception – an open, candid scrutiny of the historical record -- they discourage for a reason. Their narrative about the Holocaust is replete with unsupported

[35] Deuteronomy 20, 16-17: "... in the cities of the nations the Lord your God is giving you as an inheritance, do not leave alive anything that breathes. Completely destroy them — the Hittites, Amorites, Canaanites, Perizzites, Hivites and Jebusites -— as the Lord your God has commanded you."

claims, exaggerations, lack of evidence in the archives of the German government, and suppression of non-corroborating facts.

The Jews certainly have pushed their Holocaust narrative, but so what? Where are you going with your narrative about their narrative?

Nietzsche noted that madness, while rare in individuals, is the rule among nations. What he meant by madness was a disorder or an orientation that affects an entire people. His observation applies to Jews, too, as a people. They are collectively in a condition of madness. The form that their madness takes is psychopathological.

"Psychopathological!" That's a mouthful. What does the word mean?

It means to deal with people without scruples and without remorse, a description of Jewish behavior that applies not to their relations with each other, but to their relations with us.

With us? How is that?

This leads to the second tectonic plate in motion, ours. We European peoples also live in a condition of collective madness, which also has its roots in the past. Under the rubric of what I call the Second Synthesis, we draw upon the passions of them-and-us and high-and-low in such bizarre ways that we have undermined traditional sources of authority and now do a poor job of integrating ourselves into complex, layered hierarchies. Our madness influences how we act *vis-à-vis* our own traditions, customs, and institutions. By way of contrast, the madness of the Jews influences how they act *vis-à-vis* non-Jews. Our madness does not specifically produce psychopathology, but it does produce a social order in which the psychopaths among us meet less resistance and are able to thrive.

What difference does it make that both we and the Jews are collectively mad, but in different ways?

It makes a huge difference. Our collective madness, manifested at the level of the individual, makes us vulnerable to their collective madness, which manifests itself at the level of tribe-versus-tribe. Jeffrey Epstein's sex-entrapment operation was a prototype of this pattern, i.e., of their finding ways to bend our individual psychopaths to their tribal purpose. Many other examples of this pattern can be found. The Kennedy assassination is best understood as a collaborative effort carried out by two men, the successful, individual psychopath, Lyndon Johnson, and the successful tribe-level psychopath, Yitzhak Shamir (a man with many crimes on his resume, including the murder of Count Folke Bernadotte). We don't know whether or not Johnson collaborated with Shamir explicitly, but we do know that Johnson gave his implicit consent to the assassination of Kennedy. The evidence for Johnson's complicity lies out in the open in full view, to wit: the Warren commission report, a whitewash of the events of November 22 and strong evidence that Johnson had no interest in discovering the truth. As for 9/11, it is yet another event that can best be understood as a collaborative effort carried out by tribe-centric psychopaths in Israel and individual psychopaths in Washington.

You are saying that our madness interacts with their madness in ways that are harmful to us?

Yes, yes, this is what I am saying. However, "harmful" is too mild a word. "Devastating" is how I would put it. **The interaction of their madness with our madness filters virtuous men out of our public life, while letting toadies, sycophants, and psychopaths among us pass through to positions of power.** The process works for them. Over the decades they have consolidated so much power in the Washington government that we have become for them "a pipe to play what stop they please." The "stop" most pleasing to them for decades now has been war in the Middle East, waged by us -- at great expense to us -- for the benefit of Israel. Our subservience to their purpose pulls us away from our best traditions and is turning us into an incompetent, sycophantic, brutal, ugly, and immoral people.

This is why your second answer is "yes," the Jews are responsible for our problems?

No and yes. I say "no" because the Zionists are taking advantage of our vulnerabilities, which means answer number one continues to apply (...the fault, dear Brutus, is not in our stars, but in ourselves…etc.) However, more has to be said. To understand why I also say that "yes," the Jews **are** to be blamed for our problems, it is necessary to plumb the depths of 9/11.

What does that mean?

9/11 has to be seen not as an aberration, nor an as outlier, nor as a bolt out of the blue, but rather as one thread among many woven into the cloth of Jewish history.

How is that?

Jews have a tendency to resort to crime and violence.

How so?

Start with the *Torah.* One crucial theme of this book is Yahweh's command to the Hebrew tribes to take by violence land belonging to another tribe (and not to be squeamish about it either)? [36]

Go next to medieval times. It appears that Jews engaged in the ritual killing of Christian children in order to get Christian blood to use for ritual purposes.[37]

Next consider the October revolution in Russia. It was a Jewish conquest of the state. (Eighty percent or so of the members of Bolshevik party in 1917 were Jews). Also keep in mind that the core story of the *Torah* and the core story of Marxism resemble each other to a T. Higher authority (Yahweh in the *Torah*, History in Marxism) gives one group of people (the Hebrew Tribes in the *Torah*, the proletariat in Marxism) permission to take property (Canaan in the *Torah*, the means of production in Marxism) from another group of people (the Canaanites in the *Torah*, the bourgeoisie in Marxism). Both the *Torah* and Marxism endorse the use of violence to bring about the transfer of property. One calls the violence "Yahweh's gift to the Hebrew people;" the other calls it "revolution."

Next consider a list of political crimes committed by Jews. It is long and includes the murder of Czar Nicolas II (along with his entire family), of Lord Moyne of Britain, of Count Folke Bernadotte, of various Iranian scientists, of Shireen Abu Akeh, of Nassan Nasrallah, and of many others.[38]

---

[36] See footnote 34 or read Samuel 15: 1-35

[37] See Ariel Toaff, *Passovers of Blood: the Jews of Europe and Ritual Murder.*This book is reviewed at length in The Occidental Quarterly, Fall 2023.

[38] See Ron Unz, "Mossad Assassinations," ***The Unz Review,*** Jan.27, 2020

On a list of probable but not proven political assassinations committed by Jews, put James Forrestal, John F. Kennedy, Robert F. Kennedy, and Yassir Arafat.

Many times over the decades Israeli sharpshooters have murdered peacefully marching Palestinians, including children. They also intentionally have shot Palestinians in the knees to cripple them for life.

Under the rubric of state sponsored violence, there is "mowing the grass" in Gaza, i.e., the periodic killing of Palestinians as state policy.

Under the heading of false flag attacks, there is the King David Hotel event, the Lavron affair, the *USS Liberty* assault, and 9/11.

Under the heading of mass killing there is the assault by the Bolsheviks on the Russian aristocracy and on the clergy of the Russian Orthodox Church; there are the Sabra and Shatila massacres; and there is now the unhinged assault made by the State of Israel on the civilian population in Gaza (and in Lebanon, too).

Most of this violence committed by Jews was done to solve problems by direct action rather than by negotiation, established procedure, market transactions, or compromise. The false flag event of 9/11 was unusual only in that it was a crime of violence committed **not** against a rival or an enemy, but against us, we who have been the strongest ally and most loyal supporter of the Zionist project.

Now pause and think about 9/11. In our land, working within the institutions that we created, Jews as a people have thrived, yet even so the Zionist among them did 9/11. About this event you have to concede that it was the product of a daring and powerful imagination. It was, in fact, an event of such scope that you have to tip your hat in a grudging way to the Zionists and to the

Israelis. They pulled off a spectacular operation. However, that said, evil cannot be packaged as if it were a well-produced Hollywood spectacle. Labeling events correctly is important. **9/11 was an enormity.** They attacked us, their closest ally, in a manner that was dishonest, dishonorable, treacherous, and destructive. Besides being a gratuitous act of mass murder and an expression of contempt for us, for our institutions, and for our wellbeing as a people, 9/11 established at the heart of our political discourse a lie, to wit: that Arabs were the perpetrators of the event. Because of this lie, candid discourse in the forums of our mass media has not been possible for more than two decades. Even worse, because of this lie, the government entity in Washington has waged war throughout the Middle East against people who present no threat to us. In these wars hundreds of thousands of people have been killed and millions damaged and displaced. How do we make sense of this?

Good question. How?

A character, Nicollai Stavrogin, in one of Dostoyevsky's novels says, "... everything usually disgraceful always aroused in me an extreme delight." [39] Now consider the group of Mossad agents who on the morning of 9/11 were high fiving each other as they watched the Twin Towers belch smoke then collapse, resulting in the death of almost three thousand people. Were these Mossad agents feeling "extreme delight" due to an act made "unusually

---

[39] From the excised section of *The Possessed* by Fyodor Dostoyevsky. [Google Stavrogin's *Confession*, the excised portion of *The Possessed*, translated from the Russian by Virginia Woolf and S.S. Koteliansky, 1922]

disgraceful" by being a breach of trust so deep and twisted as to radiate with the intensity of a sort of satanic malevolence?

Perhaps.

Or, on the other hand, did 9/11 have a subtext, a deeper purpose, to wit: strengthen Jewish solidarity by committing a crime so low and so dishonorable that all Jews would be made complicit by feeling compelled to deny the crime, or cover it up, or lie about it, or use such power as they possess to suppress open and candid investigations of it?

We do not know the deep purpose of 9/11, but we do know that its immediate purpose was to further the interests of Isreal and the Zionist project. In this endeavor the operation was successful. Stories told by Jews that further their interests and that shield them from criticism are now dominant in our political arena. These stories have proved to be devastating for us. They influence our sensibilities to such an extent that we are unable to discuss, consider, or even recognize our interests as a people. The effect of these stories upon our sensibilities is why my second answer to the question – are Jews responsible for our problems -- is to say that yes, they are.

But then your third answer is "no," they are NOT the cause of our problems.

Correct. I say "no" for a reason. Jews tell stories. The emotions engendered in us by their stories are **not** something that they do to us. On the contrary, our emotional reactions to their stories are responses that we engender in ourselves. In this simple, direct way, **not** the Jews but we ourselves are the cause of our problems. In fact, I go a step further and make the following assertion: we are indebted to the Jews. They are for us a gift.

A gift?? After all that you have said, you consider them to be a gift. Are you clawing back the comments that you made a moment ago?

No, not in the least. I meant what I said a moment ago and I mean what I say now: the Jews are a gift.

In what way are they a gift?

Their domination of our public forums makes it hard for us to engage in candid discourse. To become a healthy, viable people, we have to say to the Jews "no more," which, however, is not easy. Our degree of demoralization is so profound that we now have no widespread forums among ourselves in which truth is the highest court of appeal. However, even so, we are not bereft. We have a resource that is always present and that can always be drawn upon. This resource leads to evil, hatefulness, and crime, yes, but also to patience, determination, and courage. The resource to which I refer is the human heart. This is where the Jews are forcing us to go.

To "go to the human heart" sounds good, but what does it mean?

It means to become less naïve, less innocent.[40] Can we? Do we have what it takes to become a tougher, deeper, wiser, more courageous people, or will we let ourselves be "narrated" into oblivion? Our confrontation with the Jews is a confrontation with **life**. This is the gift of the Jews. To deal with them we have to demand more of ourselves. To demand more of ourselves is an act that starts in the human heart.

Sure, but then you flip-flop again with answer number four and say that yes, the Jews are responsible for our problems?

---

[40] Keep in mind an observation made by Nietzsche: innocence is not innocent.

They have power over us. Resistance to their power begins in the individual human heart with a determined *no más,* but does not end there. Ending their power over us is an event that takes place in the political arena. To go from an individual act (a change of heart) to collective action (working together with each other in the political arena) requires that we play the game of life. To play the game of life requires that we draw upon the linking emotions of us-versus-them. To draw upon the linking emotions of us-and-them requires that we think of ourselves as a people who are worth defending. To think of ourselves as a people who are worth defending requires that we overcome confusions caused by our centuries-long embrace of contractarian narratives. It all hangs together.

How do we overcome our confusion?

Tell a different story. This is key. This is fundamental. This has to happen. This is the *sine qua non* of our recovery.

Tell a different story about what?

About lots of things, beginning with the Jews. They are masters at the game of telling stores that benefit them and damage us. (E.g.: they say that for us to work together to achieve goals that are in our interest as a people is racism.) If we want to break free of their influence, we are going to have to start telling stories that make it possible for us to play the game of life at a higher level.

How do we do that?

Get into the arena. Walk out onto the field. Do what they do: tell stories, including stories that define them.

How would you define them?

I would do so as follows: Jews = crime + anti-Semitism + never-again. That is, crime (as a solution to problems and as glue enhancing tribal solidarity) + the accusation of anti-Semitism (as a shield against blowback caused by crime) + never-again (as the foundation of a moral system). They cycle through this sequence again and again. Twenty-five years ago, they talked themselves into committing a crime that was evil and dishonorable (i.e., blowing up buildings full of people in New York City). Two years ago, they talked themselves into committing a crime that was cowardly and despicable (i.e., dropping bombs on hospitals, schools, women, and children in Gaza). Last week they talked themselves into making an unprovoked, sneak attack upon Iran. **This is who they are.**

You have made a complicated four-part answer to the question: are Jews responsible for our problems? I would like to pause long enough to pull together what you have said. Your first answer is "no," the Jews are not responsible for our problems. You state your reason for this response by citing a line from the play, Julius Caesar: "The fault, dear Brutus, is not in our stars but in ourselves that we are underlings." [41]

Your second answer is "yes," the Jews are responsible for our problems. Although you say a lot, your second answer boils down to this: they influence our sensibilities – i.e., the relationship that we have with ourselves – to such an extent that we are unable to have candid conversations among ourselves about what is in our interests as a people. This is highly destructive and potentially catastrophic.

Your third answer takes an unexpected turn. The Jews, you say, are not to be blamed for our problems. On the contrary, you consider

---

[41] Shakespeare, *Julius Caesar*, Act 1, Scene 2, line 145

them to be a gift. They bring us to a crossroads. Either we become a tougher, deeper, wiser, more courageous people, or we vanish into the (well-deserved) oblivion of undifferentiated humanity. According to you the gift of the Jews is our continuity as a people – that is to say, life -- provided that we are strong enough to impose enough discipline upon ourselves to free ourselves from their influence.

Then with answer number four you flip-flop again. The Jews, you say, are responsible for our problems. This answer, however, in my opinion, is suspect. It is cynical. Paint the Jews as a malevolent "them" – you imply -- in order to make it easier for us to form ourselves into a unified and passionate "us."

Your summary is reasonably accurate. However, I disagree with you about answer number four. We are in the game of life. The problem we face with the Jews is that they play the game without regard to scruples, honor, or integrity, a strategy that gives them advantages at first. To deal with them, we have to give ourselves permission to see them as they are.

What does that mean?

The Jews are a different people. They have a different history and a different definition of good and evil. They are now doing much damage to us. Once we let ourselves see them as they are, we can -- by drawing upon the fundamental, organizing passions of us-versus-them – put ourselves in a position to mount a collective resistance to their collective challenge. This is the game. Passion versus passion. Welcome to life. Play it or disappear. My fourth answer is not cynical. It accepts life the way it is.

The Zionists will not take our resistance lying down.

To be sure they will not. Knowledge of what they have done to us keeps them on edge. They now have us contained within a straitjacket of interwoven narrative threads. Their fear is that if one thread starts unraveling, the entire garment will unravel, leading to what would be for them a nightmare: loss of control of the narrative.

Are their fears unfounded?

No, not at all. For them to lose control of the narrative would lead to their losing control of our government's foreign policy, to their being unable to carry out crimes with impunity, and to much else, including possibly the loss of the State of Israel.

What will they do if they start losing control of the narrative?

We have already had this discussion. Crime – as a solution to problems, as a stimulant of tribal solidarity -- is their m*odus operandi.* In Russia, in Ukraine in the 1920s and 1930s, in Palestine, in New York City on 9/11, in Lebanon, in Gaza, in Beirut, and now in Iran they have shown themselves to be willing to commit crime on a scale that turns "the multitudinous seas incarnadine." They will not hesitate to do so again. They have no choice. The way they play the game leaves them exposed. The Golden Rule is a two-way street. What they have done unto others will be done unto them. They cannot afford to lose.

In order to free ourselves from their influence, should we resort to violence?

Walking down the road of cooperation requires that all parties agree to do so. Violence is different. If one party chooses the road of violence, the rest of us go down that road whether we want to or not. With 9/11 the Zionists chose violence at a level that goes beyond morality, honor, and human decency. For us to forbear in the hope that they come to their senses is proper. However, forbearance beyond a certain point leads to a loss of self-respect, of pride, and of discipline, which in turn leads to a spiraling down into vulgarity, perversity, cowardliness, and brutality.

You understand, I hope, that choosing the path of violence will cause innocent people to get hurt.

What a strange comment. "…innocent people will get hurt…." How many hundreds of thousands of innocent people have been hurt and killed because of their false flag attacks, their ginned-up wars, their dishonesty and treachery, and now their mad, indiscriminate bombing?

I mean a lot of ordinary Jews will get hurt.

I do not think that ordinary Jews will be spared from suffering the consequences of bad decisions made by their leaders (any more than we are spared from the consequences of bad decisions made by ours). As it says in their sacred book, "the fathers have eaten sour grapes and the sons' teeth are set on edge." [42] Zionist leaders chose the path of violence when they carried out the false flag attack of 9/11. Those who committed this act are evil. We have to settle scores with them. To do so without violence is possible **IF** we have access to a forum in which truth is the highest court of appeal. If no such forum can be established, then violence is the road that has to be gone down. Understand a crucial point: our failure to settle scores with them would define us **to ourselves** as men who count our manhood cheap.

[42] Jeremiah 31:29

What happens if our narratives gain traction and we start recovering our confidence?

A modified version of Gramsci.

A march through the institutions?

Yes, but I would say not so much a march through the institutions as a march overland through the counties. This is our destiny.

We have a destiny?

Yes.

If we have a destiny, we can relax. What will happen is going to happen no matter what we do.

No, wrong. Destiny is not a foreordained outcome. It is a task. If we accept the task that destiny hands to us and fail, we nevertheless will have lived lives of meaning and purpose. If we refuse the task handed to us by destiny, we may even prosper for a while, but nevertheless we will be *suicidas supervivientes.*[43]

What!!

Still living suicides.

I'm not following you.

Our task is to re-link ourselves together as a people by telling stories that engender in us the love of life. To refuse the task handed to us by destiny is to be guilty of the crime of murder. The victim of our crime, however, please understand, will not be

[43] See Ortega y Gasset, op. cit., *La Rebelión de las masas,* second footnote p.136 .

somebody else. Rather, the victim of our crime will be us, that is, a higher version of ourselves.

To reject the struggle to create a higher version of ourselves is to commit suicide even if we continue to exist? This is what you are saying?

Yes.

If we begin to emancipate ourselves from the Zionists -- and from our own native psychopaths -- what happens next?

A campaign of recovery

A recovery of what?

.... discipline, pride, willpower, leadership, narrative, morality, manhood, a version of ourselves in which stories about honor, truth, and courage engender emotions in us that influence how we act in the world. And then, of course, you could also say that no small part of what we want to recover is our land.

Our land?

Yes, our land. It has been overrun. Our task is to become the Asturians of the present age.

Asturians? Who are they? What are you talking about?

Asturias was the only part of the Iberian Peninsula not conquered by Moors. Our job is to be the Asturians of the present age and begin the long task of re-conquering what has been lost.

But all of our lands are lost.

Yes, right, which means that the first place to re-conquer has to be the realm of spirit.

Drama Number Three

The Sphere of Divinity

Divinity is a big topic. How do you define it?

My model, my simple story about a complex story, is to say that divinity and emotion are seamless and non-separable. Said another way, divinity happens in relation to emotion and circumstance.

Yeah, okay, but what does "divinity" mean all by itself?

Divinity is a story that engenders in us the strongest emotions that we are capable of feeling.

Does this mean that we create our gods by the stories that we tell?

Yes, we create our gods. To do so is unavoidable, however, proceed with caution. While we are free to create any version or vision of divinity that we want, there is a catch. We are not free to NOT create a vision of divinity. We cannot live without believing in God, or in a pantheon of gods, or in an idea or in a story that engenders in us the strongest emotions that we are capable of feeling.

You are saying that I cannot believe in nothing at all?

I suppose that what is called "depression" means having no passionate core. If you lack a passionate core, you may be alive, but you will not be vital. You will instead be a zombie, a living suicide.

If divinity is inseparable from emotion, your narrative is useless. What you are doing is trying to build a house out of water when the place where you live is in the ocean.

That's clever, but I don't think that what you say is correct. Stories engender emotion. Stories that engender in us our strongest emotions organize our sensibilities, by which I mean, they organize and structure our repertoire of emotional reactions to the world around us. We move in the direction of the gods in which we believe whether we want such movement to occur or not.

Ah, now I understand. What you are doing is extending your model of story-emotion-action to include the idea of divinity. In your world, stories about divinity give a rank ordering to the stories that we tell, which in turn give a rank ordering to the emotions that we feel, which in turn give a rank ordering to the actions that we take? We are always in a gravitational field that is organized by the gods in which we believe.

Yes. Correct. Well said. About divinity, however, a bit more is possible to say. There are moments when the sphere of divinity is experienced in a humble and elusive way. To borrow a term from athletes, it is possible to say that we are touched by divinity when we feel ourselves to be "in the zone."

I have no clue what you are talking about.

Athletes have moments when they feel themselves to be in control, while at the same time they feel themselves to be in a state of abandon. "Zoning" or being "in the zone" is what they call it. This happens not just to athletes but to all of us. Poets are in the zone when the poem on which they are working comes alive and seems to write itself. Prophets are in the zone when they feel as though their individual selves have been erased and they channel the word of God. A single individual is in the zone when he feels that he is most himself when he becomes integrated into something bigger than he is. Communities can get into the zone, e.g.,

Athens during the time of Plato and Aristotle, or Florence during the time of Rafael, Leonardo, and Michelangelo.

Entry into the zone cannot be reduced to a formula. It is teleological in the sense that getting into the zone requires goal seeking, discipline, dedication, and training. At the same time the zone is anti-teleological. Entering the zone requires relinquishing control, letting go, and being carried along in a state of abandonment. The zone is reconciliation of opposites. For athletes the opposites are control and abandon. In the case of writers, the unity of opposites is more subtle. A writer in the zone feels that his essay, book, or poem seems to be writing itself, yet at the same time he feels that what he writes while in the zone is the most profound expression of who he is.[44] The same can be said about prophets. They are in the zone when they erase themselves and feel that they have become a conduit for the word of God.

However, that said, the zone is also a source of confusion. If a prophet returns from the zone with a message about God, it is easy to assume that the message comes from God. Such is not the case. The message comes from the knowledge, wisdom, and imagination of the prophet. What comes from divinity is the passion, the flare, the controlled abandon that makes it possible for the prophet **to create out of disparate and contradictory elements a unity in the realm of narrative, passion, and action.**

---

[44] Flannery O'Connor reports that she did not know what the main event was going to be in a story that she was writing, "Good Country People," until ten or twelve lines before the main event happened. In my words (not hers) she was in the zone. The story was writing itself. See Flannery O'Connor, *Mystery and Manners*, (Farrar, Straus & Giroux, 1969) p.102--103

Your idea of divinity seems dangerous to me. Would it be okay for you to kill me if you were in the grip of a strong emotion?

From time-to-time problems arise that cannot be resolved in any other way except by violence. For this reason, violence is an alternative that cannot be discarded even though it should always be a last resort. My killing you could be heroic or dastardly depending on particulars. If I kill you for a reason that cannot be subsumed under a higher purpose, it would be dastardly.

How should we proceed with respect to the idea of divinity?

Tell the best stories we can.

About what?

Every age is different. At the present time I would say that we should be cautious about telling stories based on the idea of reason.

What is wrong with the idea of reason?

Nothing *per se*. The problem is that the idea of reason easily shades over into the belief that we can have love without the consequences of love.

What are the consequences of love?

People, more people, too many people, conflict, the game of life.

You are saying that conflict cannot be avoided?

Conflict is not a flaw of the system. It is the system. Or rather, it is half of the system. The other half is love. To speak cryptically, the system = the zone, and the zone = the reconciliation of opposites.

If we don't tell stories based on the idea of reason, what should we tell stories about?

In the present age among us, we people of and from Europe, we should tell stories about a type-man who is capable of dealing with life the way it is.

What type of man is that?

In the European tradition there exists such a man. He is celebrated in legend, ballad, narrative, and satire.

Who is he?

The knight.

You cannot be serious! What is a knight in the present age?

A man who understands that love lies at the heart of life.

What is love?

Do I have to spell that out, too? Love is a feeling of connection that is powerful, fecund, and rich in meaning and purpose -- in fact **so** powerful, **so** fecund, and **so** rich in meaning and purpose that in order for love not to extinguish itself like yeast in a Petri dish, it has to be contained. The knight understands this. He knows that love is the meaning of life, but also that love has consequences.

Consequences? What are they?

What I said just a moment ago: people, more people, too many people, conflict, the game of life.

You want us to run around in metal armor and whack each other with swords?

You are hearing me in a way that is crude. The knight knows that he has to reconcile a clash of opposites: love and the consequences of love.

This means that the knight is divided. He has deal with aspects of life that are contradictory.

Correct.

How does he deal with the problem of being divided?

He disciplines himself to live by a code, in particular the chivalric code. The discipline of living by this code is what makes him a knight.

Your answer does not tell me much.

The universal advice of the present age is "be yourself." The assumption behind this advice is that your true self lies buried under layers of convention imposed upon you by "society." This is incorrect. A reason exists why stripping away layers of convention does not reveal your true self. You do not have one. There is no such thing. There are only versions of the self, some better, some worse, some higher, some lower. The knight knows that his better self – his higher self -- is reached by fidelity to the chivalric code.

What is the chivalric code?

A code that requires a knight to be open enough and sensitive enough to give and receive love, but also to be disciplined enough, prepared enough, and brave enough to protect what -- and who -- he loves. The knight knows that if he is not prepared to protect what and who he loves, he is not and cannot be a man. He knows that he has a dual task – reconcile love and the consequences of love – which sooner or later will require of him that he swim upstream against the current of his inclinations. Discipline is where the reconciliation occurs.

There is a problem here, is there not? The knight's code is story. What happens if the story becomes corrupted?

You might be making an interesting point but say a bit more.

The knight makes something intimate -- his opinion of himself, his self-identity -- hinge upon adherence to a code. But a code is just another story circulating in the community. The knight has no control over the story as it circulates, yet depends upon it for an intimate relationship, the one that he has with himself. Is this not an example of Kierkegaardian despair? "...every life view which hinges on a condition outside itself is despair?"[45]

You are saying that the knight, because he depends on a narrative over which he has no control, is vulnerable to falling into a state of despair should his narrative become corrupted?

Yes, this is what I am saying.

What does it mean to say that a code is corrupt?

A code circulated by men who have no intention of following it is corrupt. Consider the American military, for example, an organization with a high-minded code of honor, which code, however, is

---

[45] Kierkegaard, Soren, *Either/Or*, vol. II, Princeton University Press and Doubleday Anchor Books, Garden City, N.Y., 1959. p.240

now little more than a façade behind which the leaders of the military run riot in an orgy of greed, of corruption, of brutality against the weak, and of a cowardly subservience to power (including a foreign power).

I agree that the knight depends upon honest discourse. However, the problem of honest discourse is ubiquitous. All of us (we human creatures) set ourselves in motion based on feelings engendered by the stories that we hear and tell. However, I do not think that it is accurate to say that the knight depends completely on a story that is beyond his control.

How so?

You and I are not two different people. Rather, we are one person talking in two different voices. Our discourse, because it is under our control, can be as honest as we know how to make it. This does not mean that we have special access to truth, but it does mean that we can tell a story that has as much integrity as we are capable of achieving by honesty, by attentiveness to subtle flows of emotion, and by a disciplined scrutiny of ourselves as we act in the world.

If I have the capacity to set myself in motion based on stories that I tell to myself, what stops me from telling stories in which the only consideration of importance to me is my self-interest crudely defined. That is, what stops me from falling into the abyss of psychopathology?

Your desire to be part of something bigger than you are…

What do you mean?

The psychopath restricts his horizon to the confines of his primate gang. He sees and responds to the terror of life, but not to its majesty and beauty. Opening himself to the beauty and majesty of life would reduce the intensity of his attachment to his primate gang, thereby making him vulnerable. What this means is that the psychopath has to deny his higher self. (As a parenthetical aside, this is what Ortega meant by the word "revolt" in his book, *The Revolt of the Masses.* A man becomes a mass-man when he revolts against his higher self).

What is the point that you are trying to make?

I am trying to describe the knight as an ideal. He is a man who is not in state of rebellion against himself. He knows that attaining a higher vision of himself means moral and spiritual integration into a community. He knows that integration into a community requires narrative, tradition, art, discipline, and hierarchy – i.e. culture -- all of which he respects and honors. Ah, but there is something else, something additional, that the knight also knows, that culture has to be subordinate to nature. Here is where we (the so-called Best) have gone astray. We want an "us" without a "them." This is not possible. "Them" is an unavoidable part of the discipline of life. To deny "them" is to give ourselves an excuse to be undisciplined and therefore unprepared to defend who and what we love. What results from our not defending who and what we love is that we grow to hate ourselves and lose the capacity to love. What the chivalric code accomplishes is train, organize, and channel – but not extirpate – the passions of life. **The discipline of the chivalric code makes it possible for us to live with passionate intensity in a world of them-and-us without cutting ourselves off from the majesty and beauty of life.**

(Or you can make this same point going in the opposite direction. The chivalric code makes it possible to be open to the majesty and beauty of life while yet being disciplined enough to accept and deal with – and not fall into a state of denial about -- the implacable world of them-and-us.)

If I were to agree with you and decide to pursue the ideal of being a knight, I would feel like a phony, or a man in a condition of arrested adolescence, or a genial kook wandering around the countryside looking for windmills to tilt against. How is it possible to return to an archaic ideal without being ridiculous?

Consider your life to be a training regimen, the purpose of which is to prepare yourself to give love, to receive love, and to deal with the consequences of love. Of the three, my personal opinion is that what is hardest to achieve for us now (we men of the present age) is to feel that we deserve to be loved. This is because we are not defending what we love.

What stories do I tell to train myself to be a knight?

We have already discussed this topic. For now, it means that you stop telling stories based on the idea of reason. Too easily do such stories introduce a false hope, to wit: that the right philosophy, the right institution, the right technology, the right church, or the right political movement will make it possible to have love without the consequences of love. T. S. Eliot says:

> The last temptation is the greatest treason
> To do the right deed for the wrong reason.[46]

I disagree with Eliot on this point. The greatest treason is to think that it is possible to have love without valor.

---

[46] TS Eliot. *Murder in the Cathedral*

It always seems to come down to love in your view of the world.

Yes, love = life.

Please spare me from another one of your corny equations. If love = life, and if life = the zone, and if the zone = the reconciliation of opposites, then life = a jumble of contradictions.

Yes, yes exactly. That's what life is – a jumble of contradictions – which is why our lives and communities cannot rest on a foundation of logic. Life and community have to be based on stories that produce emotions that reconcile love and the consequences of love, or -- to say this a bit more abstractly -- that reconcile the beauty of life with the terror of life.

Why can't we love all of mankind?

Meditate on the example of Jean Jacque Rousseau.

Jean Jacque Rousseau?? Why do you mention him?

He is an example....

... of what...?

.... of what happens when you refuse to subordinate your culture to nature.

You'll have to explain what you mean by that.

Rousseau considered his own children to be a burden and put them in an orphanage for foundlings, where they may well have died of neglect. The intoxication of his vision was so strong that whether or not his own children lived or died was of less importance to him than the glorious task that he set for himself of being a midwife attending to the birth of a new age of man.

What is it that you are saying about Rousseau?

I am saying about him what Edmund Burke said about him: "he exhausted the stores of his powerful rhetoric in the expression of a universal benevolence, while his heart was incapable of one common spark of parental affection."[47]

Rousseau was just one man. How can you draw conclusions based on a sample of one?

His flaws as an individual are our flaws as a people. We are destroying our children as effectively as he destroyed his.

Your language is unhinged. How are we destroying our children?

By letting our country become overrun with strangers, by destroying the beauty of our land, by turning our cities into cesspools of moral and aesthetic degradation, by telling feral children to "be themselves" (thereby setting them up to become sociopaths and psychopaths), by making political capital out of sterile sexual practices, by depriving our children of beauty, elegance, and hierarchy, by failing to give to our children a sense of themselves as a proud people with high standards and much to accomplish, et cetera. The list of the ways that we fail our children is long and dismal, yet even so most of the entries on the list have their origins in one condition, a lack of valor.

---

[47] Burke, Edmond, *Reflections on the Revolution in France*. Op.cit. p.271

I'll have to think about what you say. In the meantime, I am going to change the subject. What do you think about the Christian religion?

This **is** a change of subject. You want me to get into trouble by offering an opinion on Christianity?

Yes.

I'll tell you what I think but understand, what I offer is opinion.

Of course it is. We know that. Stop making excuses and do your job of answering questions.

I didn't know my job was to answer questions.

It's your role in this drama. Play it.

A Note on Christianity

Christianity is not the story *per se* about Christ told in the New Testament, but rather the emotion that the story engenders.

To say this is not surprising, given your so-called "model."

The question I ask is as follows: can a story told two thousand years ago engender the same emotions and issue forth into the same actions now compared to then? My answer is no, probably not. Too much has happened.

How so?

Two thousand years ago, and even within the last three centuries or so, Christians believed in the details of their New Testament story. The strength of their belief made it possible for them to create institutions that shaped the sensibilities of each new generation.

Now, however, the continuity of Christianity has been altered and interrupted. Narratives from science, secular history, and evolution -- having nothing directly to do with the Christian story – have, nevertheless, even so, had an effect. These narratives have weakened the emotional reaction of Christians to their New Testament story whether they want this to happen or not. What Christians do now is rely on sentimentality, meaning: their **desire** to believe the Christian story is for them a sufficient reason to proclaim that they **do** believe the Christian story.

This sentimentalism.... what is it?

It is when you believe that X is true because you want to believe that X is true. Non-sentimental belief, on the other hand, is to believe that X is true whether you want it to be true or not? The distinction is subtle but important. It has two major consequences.

How so?

In earlier times Christian belief led to the creation of Christian institutions (cathedrals, churches, ecclesiastical structures, educational institutions, religious orders, military orders, etc.) that did the work of forming the sensibilities of the next generation. These institutions were supported by belief in the Christian story. Then science, secular history, and the idea of evolution appeared on the scene and changed the emotional relationship of Christians to their story, thus of necessity to their institutions. What is happening now is that Christianity is NOT supported by people who believe that the Christian story is true whether they want it to be or not. Rather, Christianity is supported by people who want to believe in the story. These people have a deep legacy of Christian institutions to draw upon that facilitate being and acting like Christians. However, there is a problem. One consequence of

Christianity being supported by sentiment (rather than by what we think is true whether we want it to be true or not) is that these Christian institutions become vulnerable to capture.

Capture means what?

Christians, like many other European peoples, are drawn to the emotions that are engendered by Second Synthesis stories. Meanwhile, as just discussed, the vitality of Christianity has been reduced by narratives about science and evolution. The result is that many Christians now try to incorporate Second Synthesis narratives into their Christian story in order to feel the emotions that these Second Synthesis narratives are capable of engendering. This leads to accretions to Christian belief and to strange amalgamations of Christian practice, e.g., Christianity as socialism sanctioned by Jesus, Christianity as straight-up Marxism (liberation theology), Christianity as group therapy; Christianity as a foundation for market success, and many other variations, including the strangest of all, but also one of the most instructive of all, Christianity as Christian Zionism.

Christian Zionism instructive? An end-times cult that wants the Jews to build a Third Temple on the site in Jerusalem where now stands the Al-Aqsa Mosque so that THEY, the Christians, can be carried off to the next world. Far from being instructive, this is yet another example of collective madness.

You have not understood my point. Christian Zionism is instructive because it is a symptom of disarray. So little do Christian Zionists love life that they tell stories about being whisked away from it. To use their term, they want to be "raptured." Pause for a moment and contemplate the strange idea of rapture, especially in terms of Nietzsche's retrospective inference.[48] What is it about Christian Zionists that causes them to be drawn to the idea of rapture? How is the desire to be erased from life anything but nihilism, even if the erasure happens gently and you end up in heaven?

You think that Christian Zionism is a form of nihilism?

Yes, I do. In addition, as if not already strange enough, these Christian Zionists, while waiting for the rapture to occur, identify with Jews, a people not shy about going after what they want. Like waifs out in the cold, Christian Zionists seek warmth by huddling close to the heat of Jewish fire. They want to feel vicariously, in a manner that is permissible, the emotions of them-and-us that burn so intensely in the Jewish heart.

What should these strange Christians do – indeed, what should all Christians do?

Come home. Heat themselves by the warmth of their own fire. Link Christianity to biological communities of ethnic Europeans. Make Christianity ethnocentric.

Why?

Once the vitality of their religion began to be sapped by science and evolution, Christians found themselves drawn to Second Synthesis stories, especially Marxism. They now have a tendency

---

[48] "...my vision has always become keener in tracing that most difficult and insidious of all forms of retrospective inference, ...the inference from the work to the author, ... from the ideal to him who needs the ideal, from every form of thinking and valuing to the desire behind it" Nietzsche, *The Joyful Wisdom*, #370, in *The Philosophy of Nietzsche*, edited by Geoffrey Clive, (A Mentor Book, New York,1965.) p.538

to judge the value of their religion by political criteria. To be sure, Second Synthesis sentiment can be found in Scripture. ("I say to you, as you did it to one of the least of these, my brothers, you did it to me.").[49] [50] However, Christians are naïve about the Second Synthesis. They do not understand that it introduces into our lives a deep instability.

The Second Synthesis introduces into our lives a deep instability …?? Once again, I have no clue what you are talking about.

For three centuries we people of and from Europe have used contractarian, Second Synthesis, OUGHT TO BE stories to organize ourselves politically. Over the centuries these stories have led to a series of type-men, one emerging after the other.

The series begins with:

The man of tradition. His ideas as well as his sensibilities are shaped by tradition. His problem is inflexibility.

Next comes the high point of the Second Synthesis, a type-man who embraces Second Synthesis ideas while he yet retains the sensibilities and morals of his Christian heritage. His embrace of new ideas gives him mental flexibility. His legacy of morality and sensibility from his Christian past make it possible for him to live a moral life in a coherent social order. The combination of mental flexibility and social coherence leads to men and women who are flexible, moral, disciplined, productive, and sometimes fabulously creative.

---

[49] Mathew 25-41

[50] Gomez-Davila, aphorism number 2971. "The progressive Christian's error lies in believing that Christianity's perennial polemic against the rich is an implicit defense of socialist programs." https://don-colacho.blogspot.com/2011/03/2943.htm

Next on the scene comes mass-man. Both his ideas and his sensibilities are formed by Second Synthesis ideology. He wants rights of every sort but feels no sense of solidarity with the people on which his wellbeing depends, (hence no understanding of what **they** have to have for **him** to be able to count upon them).

Linked to mass man is socialist man. This type-man exists across the width and breadth of the Second Synthesis. He gets his categories of them-and-us and high-and-low from political discourse. He can be a communist, a classical socialist, a libertarian, or anything in between.

Next comes primate-man. What defines this type-man is an inability to integrate himself into complex hierarchical structures. He responds socially only to matters that touch him at the gang level of emotion and coercion. Though a type-man who has been around forever, he is now flourishing. All too frequently he and his gang end up at the top of the political mountain.

Next comes antifa-man, a type-man stripped of his past except for one crucial aspect of it, to wit: the incoherence that lies at the heart of the Second Synthesis. This incoherence he has assimilated so completely that it forms the core of his identity. The incoherence of antifa-man is this: in the name of tolerance, he is intolerant; in the name of being a champion of the poor, he damages the poor; in the name of equality, he exacerbates inequality; in the name of opposing racism against blacks, he endorses racism against whites; in the name of being against hatred, he hates; in the name of love, he hates those who do not love as he thinks they ought to love. Because he is what he proclaims to abhor, he cannot engage in debate lest he come to see himself as he is. Given that he organizes his life around a narrative that leads to emotional incoherence, you might think that he would be the last man in the series of type-men produced by the Second Synthesis. Such is not the case.

Now appearing on stage is transgender-man, or rather transgender-person. If transgender-person is a man, in order to make himself into a victim, he proclaims himself to be a woman. If transgender-person is a woman, in order to make herself into a victim, she proclaims herself to be a man. Surely these type-people are the end of the line. After the mutilation that they visit upon themselves psychologically and sometimes physically, what can come next except suicide?

(As a parenthetical aside, I cannot refrain from suggesting that you compare this seven, eight, or nine generation history of instability with the one thousand generations during which our cave dwelling ancestors passed down an artistic tradition of a degree of complexity not matched in some respects – having to do with perspective -- until Renaissance Italy.)

Why are you telling me about the Second Synthesis? I thought we were talking about Christianity.

In so far as Christians seek to feel emotions engendered by Second Synthesis narratives, they put themselves on a path that leads to fragmentation, instability, incoherence, and self-destruction. Rather than trying to tap into the unstable emotions of the Second Synthesis, I suggest that Christians dedicate themselves to overcoming its destructive effects.

How?

By telling stories that link their religion to "us."

So, it is back to the idea of ethnocentrism....

Yes.

Do you think an ethno-centric narrative would be viable for us, we people of and from Europe?

Yes, very much would such a narrative be viable. To gain a sense of the power of stories about ourselves as a people, look at the efforts made by the psychopaths at the top of the state to stop us, we European peoples, from telling stories that advance our interests as a people. These psychopaths want to establish in us a false consciousness, meaning: they want us to tell stories, engender emotions, and take actions that serve their interests not ours. In particular they want us to tell stories that support the state (the source of their power) rather than to tell stories that support us as a people.

I am unclear about what an ethnocentric version of Christianity implies. Would non-Euro people, Africans, for example, or any other people, be excluded from your Euro-Christian communities? I ask because if this is what you have in mind, I can assure you that many Christians would feel uncomfortable -- no, outrage – no, horror -- at your suggestion. St. Paul is explicit on this topic. "There is neither Jew nor Greek...slave nor free...male and female. You are all one in Christ Jesus." [51]

It is not that European peoples, and African peoples cannot believe in the same god. Certainly, they can. The problem is that the two peoples are different. Not so long ago, whites enslaved blacks. Now in the present age blacks are engaged in a low level, spontaneous assault on white people and their institutions. Differences between the two peoples of temperament, style, and patterns of morality and rationality are deeply rooted.

---

[51] *[Galatians 3:28]*

What is the problem?

We human beings are the problem. Our minds -- far from being programmable via an operating system called "the logos" -- are a repertoire of emotions, proclivities, contradictory tendencies, and strong and weak points, all of which differ from individual to individual, but also in systematic ways from people to people. It is hard for Europeans and Africans to live together without subordination of one to the other. Since neither party wants to be subordinate, the outcome is a state of tension that gives an advantage to one particular type-man, the psychopath and his gang.

The solution is for European Christians to come home?

Yes. They should come home. The time is propitious.

Propitious? In what way?

Galileo's discovery that moons revolve around Jupiter caused a strong reaction against him on the part of the Church. Darwin's ideas about evolution caused strong negative reactions against him on the part of many Protestants. Now, in the present age, data about differences among the tribes and races of mankind are **not** confirming basic tenets of Second Synthesis ideology (about equality, about the influence of nature versus nurture, etc.). The response made to the data is an angry reaction of denial. However, for once, the leaders of this angry reaction tend not to be Christians, but Zionists, Marxists, socialists, crony capitalists, and bureaucrats. Their reaction is so strong and so defensive that it might well be an indication that the centuries-long tide of the Second Synthesis has finally begun to crest. If so, then the moment is propitious. Let the Zionists, the socialists, the crony capitalists, and the bureaucrats expend themselves trying to hold back the receding flow of an ebbing Second Synthesis tide. The time for European Christians to come home is now.

Come home means what...?

... that European Christians champion European peoples and that European Christians insist upon integrity in the search for truth....

If Christians were to take these steps, they would trigger strong reactions.

You better believe they would. My guess is that if European Christians were to come home, they would be surprised by the vehemence of two waves of reaction. The first wave would be a torrent of vitriol and violence directed against them by Zionists, by socialists, by crony capitalists, by bureaucrats, and by no small number of their fellow Christians. The second wave would take time to emerge. However, were it to gather strength, it would generate a surge of support from us, we European peoples, as we begin waking up in the dawn of a new day and start realizing the degree to which we had been living through a long, dark night of the soul.

What would an ethnocentric revision of Christianity look like?

Christians will have to answer that question. I can only say what I would like to see them do.

What?

I said earlier that two major consequences occur when Christians base their religion on what they **want to be true** rather than on what they think is true whether they want it to be true or not. One consequence, already mentioned, is that Christianity based on sentimentality makes Christian institutions vulnerable to capture by storytellers who tell stories that we think are true whether we want the stories to be true or not.

There is a second consequence. When Christians believed that Jesus existed (whether they wanted him to or not), their belief was not an isolated occurrence. Rather, their belief in Jesus was embedded in a worldview. Included in this worldview was the belief that a force for evil exists in the world. This had implications. Were Christians to flout the good, they would risk falling into the hands of a divine manifestation of the bad. In the context of the times, their belief in Jesus was a source of discipline.

Now fast forward to the present.

Modern Christians believe in Jesus because they want to. Ah, but do they also want to believe in a divine manifestation of the bad, i.e., in Satan? No, not so much. Herein lies the second danger of basing belief on desire. To want to believe in Jesus -- but not in Satan -- makes it easy for modern Christians to turn their religion into a form of escape, that is, into a vision of good with no vision of evil. This takes them off the hook. They do not have to discipline themselves to face the dark side of life, **including the dark side of themselves.** To refuse to see evil in others is dangerous; to refuse to see evil in ourselves is fatal. The distance between modern Christians and classical socialism is paper thin. Very similar forces are at work. Both groups are complacent about the moral superiority of their good intensions.

(Finally, as a parenthetical aside, let me note that in the case of Christian Zionism, matters are a bit different. Christian Zionists have no permissible "them." In order to secure a "them," they consider the enemies of Zion to be their enemies, a strategy that works, but at a cost. Christian Zionists secure for themselves a well-defined "them." The cost of their strategy is that their understanding of "us" becomes muddled and confused. They do not know where they stop and the Jews start, a lack of clarity that makes them vulnerable to being manipulated by the Jews, who in matters having to do with boundaries are crystal clear.)

You have given me a lot of background, but you have not told me what you would like for Christians to do.

I would like for European Christians to re-introduce discipline into their religion by connecting themselves to us, we people of and from Europe. Like all people we are struggling to survive on the dense and crowded surface of planet earth. In identifying with us as a people, Christians could learn much from the Jews about links between a people and their religion (provided these Christians do not conflate their interests with the interests of the Jews and provided that they do not fall off the donkey on the other side as the Jews have done[52]).

I would like Euro-Christians to stop judging themselves by how well they reach Second Synthesis political goals (equality, justice as fairness, etc.) and instead judge themselves by the vitality of their people, the beauty of their towns, the elegance of their manners, the spiritual depth of their art, and the health, vigor, variety, and beauty of the natural world in which they live and on which they depend.

I would like for European Christians to let go of the seductive notion that religion is a universal solvent capable of dissolving

[52] Attributed to Martin Luther: mankind is like a drunken peasant; you push him up one side of the donkey and he falls off the other.

differences among peoples, nations, and tribes. There is no way to avoid the hardest task that we face, which is to have to live in a closed system – in a Petri dish -- on the surface of planet earth with **the other**, i.e., with people who have different manners, different interests, different histories, different genetic inheritances, and different definitions of good and evil. The pressure of living in a Petri dish is not an aberration of life, **it is life.** All living creatures have to face it and deal with it

I would like for European Christians to accept the inevitability of conflict. This means that they have to have a leader who can deal in the medium of violence. Such leaders, however, **always** come with a high price tag. They **always** have an incentive to gin up conflict in order to increase personal and political power. No way exists to escape this dilemma. However, size helps. In small sovereign units it is easier to know the following: when a political leader is veering off track, who can be trusted to stand with you in opposition to the leader, and what levers, ropes, and pulleys are available to push, pull, or drag the leader back on track -- or get rid of him.

I would like for Christians to consider words spoken by Shatov, a character in Dostoyevsky's novel, *The Possessed*:

> "... he who has no people has no God. You may be sure that all who cease to understand their own people and lose their connection with them, at once lose at the same time the faith of their fathers and become atheistic or indifferent."[53]

Let me make an addition to Shatov's comment based on a few more years of history. A people who have lost their connections to

[53] Dostoevsky, Fyodor https://www.gutenberg.org/cache/epub/8117/pg8117-images.html#H2CH0006 Chapter 11, part VII (translated by Constance Garnett).

each other may pass through a phase of indifference and atheism, but atheism and indifference do not mark the end of the road. Once connections are lost among a people, they become vulnerable to being captured by a psychopath and his tightly-linked gang. **This** is the end of the road.

And finally, I would like for Christians – and all the rest of us, too – to think about the link that exists between divinity and passion.

What are you talking about?

If emotion and divinity make a seamless whole (as I assume), and if stories about divinity elicit in us the strongest emotions that we are capable of feeling, this leads to a question: what actions do we take based on our stories about divinity? Where do our stories about divinity take us?

That's an easy question to answer. If our vision of divinity is good, we will be drawn towards the good. If our vision of divinity is bad, we will be drawn towards the bad.

Ah, yes, I thought you would answer my question as you did, which is why I asked it the way I did. I apologize for manipulating you just the least little bit. In my opinion, your understanding of divinity is incorrect. You see the divine as a force drawing us towards itself. If our vision of divinity is good, we are drawn towards the good or, on the other hand, if our vision is bad, we are drawn towards the bad. I see matters differently. In my view divinity and passion are non-separable. What this means is that the same story can have us going towards good or towards evil. This is because the potential for good and evil lies within us. From inside our story, it is not possible to know in which direction we are going. To gain a sense of direction we have to have a reference point that lies outside the story. In my opinion such a reference point exists and is capable of providing orientation, at least after the fact. The reference point to which I refer is beauty. Movement towards divine good leads to beauty. Movement towards divine evil leads to ugliness. That's my synthesis.

A synthesis of what?

… of individual and culture, of culture and nature, of nature and divinity……

Why does beauty seem to be linked to the good?

Beauty is the unknowable depth of the self in sync with the unknowable depth of nature. When the individual is subordinate to his culture and when his culture is subordinate to nature, the unknowable depth of the individual and the unknowable depth of nature are in sync. Part and whole are in harmony.

What about the psychopath and his gang? Are they in sync with nature?

Were the psychopath a chimpanzee, then yes, he and his troop would be subordinate to nature and therefore part of the beauty of nature. But the psychopath is not a chimpanzee. He is a man. When he restricts his more ample consciousness to the confines of a primate gang, he is out of sync with the full range of awareness of which he is capable, hence out of sync with the unknowable depth of himself as a living creature, hence out of sync with the unknowable depth of nature. He realizes his interests as a living creature **not** by integration into the whole, but at the expense of the whole. This leads to ugliness and vulgarity.

What is vulgarity?

It is what results when we listen to, tell, and act on stories that are below the level of awareness of which we are capable. To do this consciously is to be in a state of rebellion against our higher self.

Where are we now as a people?

Look around. Contemplate our land, our landscape, our art, our manners, our dress, our physiques, our "lifestyles" -- and tell me what you see.

I won't deny it. I see a lot of ugliness.

This tells us something about the direction in which we are going, don't you think?

I suppose it does, but not every aspect of contemporary life is ugly.

For sure. Don't forget, we have to understand what is happening to us via models, i.e., via simple stories about complex stories. Our stories do not and cannot account for everything. In addition, of course, we cannot escape from either the prison of narrative or from the prison of having to live in the eternal present. However, even so, nevertheless, we can remember and model the past and we can refine our sensibilities by creating and letting ourselves be influenced by high art, i.e., by the best that has been said, thought, and pictured. To be influenced by high art improves our ability to make distinctions in the present between the beautiful and the vulgar, on the basis of which we can take steps -- however modest

– in the direction of a goal that we are a long way from reaching, but that we will have to reach if we are going to survive as a species.

What goal is that....?

... integration of consciousness into the web of life. This happens (according to my model) when the dominant stories that we tell lead to actions the outcomes of which are beautiful.

Section Two

Definitions, Elucidations, Applications,

Two Letters, and Two Dramas

Introduction

Section two is philosophical housekeeping. Words, phrases, and ideas are defined and discussed – or further defined and further discussed. Two more dramas are included, and two letters are written, one to our women and the other to us, we men of and from Europe. The basic model is adhered to throughout (narrative engenders emotion and of emotion issues forth into action). The agenda remains the same (change the actions that we take by changing the stories that we tell). The commitment to truth also remains the same.

To say that I am committed to truth sounds pretentious and even pointless. If I were not committed to truth, I would have no qualms about stating that I was, so why go through the exercise? First and foremost because words matter. When I say that I am committed to truth, my words are directed to myself. A commitment to truth has two imperatives: 1) do not let fear, pusillanimity, social coercion, or political correctness stop me from saying what I think is true. But also 2): do not let rigidity, vanity, neurosis, or pride stop me from being open to the possibility that somebody else might be telling a better story. A commitment to truth is a commitment to discourse. Since discourse is something that happens in a community, to be committed to truth is to be committed to a community in which truth is the highest court of appeal.

Definitions

Philosophers of a school of thought called "idealism" argue that human beings do not have direct access to the external world, but access only to ideas in their minds about the external world. Numerous problems beset this school of thought, not the least of which is that its members have not been able to establish a stable narrative line. The Spanish philosopher, Ortega y Gasset, avoids the problems of idealism by making no distinctions between an inner and an outer world. His starting point is "*yo soy yo y mi circumstancia*" ("I am me and my circumstance").

I concur with Ortega, which means that I think the following: 1) we exist in the circumstance, 2) the circumstance is bigger than we are, 3) the circumstance is bigger than we can imagine it to be, 4) we have to deal with the circumstance if we want to keep on living in it, and 5) dealing with the circumstance requires orientation, and orientation means telling stories about who we are, where we are, what we have to do, what we should do, et cetera.

No story told from inside the circumstance can encompass it. To deal with the circumstance requires models and maps.

> A *model* = a simple story about a complex story.
> A map = a simple picture of a complex picture.

Maps and models, though always inadequate, are also always unavoidable. A complex story cannot be acted upon. Too much information and too many contingencies have to be considered. Action requires that choices be made about what is and what is not important. If no model is explicitly acted upon, it is nevertheless the case that a model is implicit in any action that we take.

Human Action

According to popular speech (and according to what could be called the "standard model" among those of us in the European tradition) there are two triggers to human action: emotion and reason. This model is defective. It tells no story *ex ante* about how we act on reason instead of emotion or vice-versa, which means that the rationality of a decision cannot be determined beforehand. It can only be determined after we find out whether or not a decision that we made turned out to be a good one.

An Alternative Model of Human Action

(Used in these Essays)

Three words constitute the starting point of an alternative model of human action: "circumstance," "creature" and "emotion." Because these words are the first words of the model, they cannot be defined by the model. Their meaning has to be assumed. "Circumstance" and "creature" involve intuitive assumptions. "Emotion" is a bit more difficult.

Circumstance is where we exist and where we have to make our way if we want to keep on existing.

Creatures are living entities that draw upon emotion to do what all living creatures have to do: make their way in the circumstance.

Emotion is harder to define. The word comes from Latin "*e*," out of or from, plus *movere,* to move, which would seem to indicate that the Romans understood emotion to be a process by which we set ourselves in motion and act in the world. I concur with the Romans on this matter. Emotion is feeling and acting. The two are inseparable. However, they have to be separated in order to define the word "emotion." What this means is that the definition of the word is already a model, already a simple story about a complex story.

Ideas

Ideas are explicit, implicit or condensed narratives that engender emotion on the basis of which we act in the circumstance. The core assumption of these essays is that we tell stories, that these stories engender emotions, and that these emotions issue forth into action.

Reason and Nature

The idea of reason as a separate or special faculty of the human mind is rejected, which, however, does not mean that thinking is rejected. Thinking is telling stories to determine what an emotional reaction of ours should be. Many specialized kinds of stories – logic, mathematics, etc. – are useful. If you want to use the word "reason" to describe the steps that are taken in order to determine what an emotional reaction should be, fine, go ahead, be my guest, but understand what is happening. To say that a bad decision is based on emotion rather than on reason is misleading. Bad decisions based on bad thinking (i.e., bad story telling) happen all the time, but saying that bad decisions happen because passion trumps reason adds nothing to the discussion. Without a story about how or why reason is selected instead of passion, or vice-versa, the word "reason" is just another way to say "good," or "I approve" or "it turned out to be the right decision."

Nature

The idea of nature is not rejected. 1) Nature is observed regularities in the circumstance (e.g., water freezes at zero degrees centigrade at sea level on planet earth). 2) Nature is also the totality of living things unfolding together through time, across the generations, on the surface of planet earth, interacting with each other and taking advantage of each other and being constrained by each other and by the regularities (or the lack of regularities) in the circumstance.

Magic and Reason

Magic is the use of incantations and ritual to attempt to circumvent the limitations of nature. "Reason" in the present age has a meaning close to the meaning of the word "magic" but with this difference: where magic uses incantation and ritual to try to circumvent nature, reason uses logic and mathematics to attempt the same thing.

The Idea of Reason and the Idea of Heaven

People use the idea of reason to tell stories about how to make life less harsh, more bountiful and more secure. To want to do so is understandable. However, there are problems with the idea. Keeping in mind what Nietzsche called the "backward inference" gives cause for concern. European peoples, once no longer touched emotionally by Christian stories about heaven, were drawn to stories about reason as a replacement. However, not surprisingly, replacing stories about heaven with stories about reason has consequences. The idea of heaven in the old Christian dispensation was a refuge, but not an escape. It engendered emotions that encouraged people to stay in the game of life, plugging away, facing the difficulties that had to be faced until the arrival of a day of reckoning. The idea of reason, on the other hand, in the new dispensation of the Second Synthesis, is also a refuge, but one that works on a different plan. Promising much and delivering much, the idea of reason encourages people to think that they have now, or that they soon will have a solution to problems. However, there is a difficulty with the idea of reason. What happens when a problem arises that cannot be dealt with except by measures that are unfair, inequitable, or conducive to conflict? The idea of reason in such cases offers no solution. It has to be set aside or given up on. However, to give up on an idea that is a source of solace and orientation is hard to do. Faced with problems that cannot be solved except by measures that are unreasonable, all too often people who believe in the idea of reason take refuge in denial, which, of course, is no solution. A problem denied does not go away. Rather it is handed over to somebody else. In the present age this "somebody else" invariably turns out to be men who control the state.

Denial and Rank

Denial may occur in complicated ways but at its core it is simple and intuitive. A man wants to fly to New York. As he contemplates the prospect of flying, a fragment off narrative occurs to him, "planes crash from time to time." This fragment of narrative engenders in him the emotion of fear. Were he to do nothing about it, his fear of flying would prevail over his desire to fly. He deals with the problem of fear by telling himself a second story, "flying is safer than driving." This second story engenders an emotion in him on the basis of which he denies his fear of flying and goes out to the airport.

"Denial," however, may not be the most accurate word to use to describe the process. Rather than denial, what is happening to the man is that he is subordinating one narrative ("planes crash from time to time") to another narrative ("flying is safer than driving"). Making possible this act of subordination is a third narrative, such as, for example, a story that he tells to himself about himself: "I am not the type of man who lets himself be daunted by considerations of fear." This third more abstract narrative establishes an order of rank among the narratives that occur to him, on the basis of which he makes a choice and sets himself in motion.

The power of narrative to establish an order of rank among the stories that we tell -- hence among the emotions that we feel, hence among the actions that we take -- is impressive. The power that comes from being able to establish a dominant narrative is vast.

Social Coercion, Peer Pressure

Social coercion is the pressure that we feel to do what *is done* or to not do what is *not done*. Another way to say, "social coercion" is to say, "peer pressure." José Ortega y Gasset says the following about the word "social":

> "I have said about our world, that in so far as it is 'social,' it is one of permanent and universal coercion."[54]

What he meant is not quite as bad as it sounds:

> "Let us say formally that there is coercion whenever we cannot decide to do with impunity anything other than what 'is done' in the collective." [55]

In other words, if I do something that is *not done*, I can expect an emotional reaction of disapproval on the part of people around me. This disapproval may be mild. However, if I persist in doing a thing that is *not done*, the level of disapproval becomes progressively more intense. Silent disapproval gives way to vocal disapproval, which in turn gives way to ostracizing me, which in turn gives way to taking steps to inflict economic damage on me. At

[54] Ortega y Gasset, *Obras Completas* ,Tomo VII p. 236
[55] Ortega y Gasset, *Obras Completas* Tomo VII p.236

the highest level of severity, if I persist in doing a thing that is *not done*, violence may be directed against me with impunity. (A contemporary variation of this extreme level of social coercion is to anathematize me in the public media, while leaving acts of violence to goons, mobs, political extremists, unscrupulous DAs, careless swat teams, or people of shaky mental stability.)

Manners and Usages

Social coercion is conveyed through narratives, manners and usages.

Manners are deliberate gestures that we make with each other that signal membership in or standing within a group.

Usages are stories, gestures, words, and symbols that generate an involuntary emotional reaction. If you see me do action X, for example, or hear or read about me doing X, and you have an emotional reaction of approval or disapproval, then X is a usage. How X becomes linked to emotional reactions is similar to or perhaps identical with the way that language is learned

Usages, Emotion, Action

Emotional reactions engendered by usages are involuntary. We have them whether we want to or not. Action, on the other hand, is different. We can choose to act or not act on an emotional reaction. Suppose, for example, that action A is an action that is *not done*. If, even so, we decide to do action A, we have to face two sources of anxiety. One is self-generated and comes from telling stories to ourselves using the pronoun "they." What will *they* think? What will *they* say? What will *they* do? If we overcome the self-induced anxiety of they-stories and do what is *not done*, we then have to face the actual, negative reactions of others.

A Social Order.

The accumulation of social capital leads to a social order, defined as *a group of people with coherent emotional reactions to each other.* What this means is that individuals in their various capacities, roles, and stations in life have emotional reactions to each other that are complementary. This complementarity makes it possible for them to work together in some degree of harmony.

Sensibility.

A dominant narrative that is carried along from one generation to the next imparts a commonality to the taste, style, speech, movement and gestures of the people who tell and act upon the narrative. This commonality is "sensibility."

The sensibilities of one generation come from the dominant narratives, emotions, and actions of previous generations. Like one's native language, sensibility is acquired while growing up. It can be thought of as our most intimate relationship, the one that we have with ourselves.

Language and sensibility are similar. The older we are, the harder it is to learn to speak a different language. Likewise, the older we are the harder it is to acquire a different repertoire of sensibilities. However, to change the sensibilities of an entire people does not require a bulldozer. A change can occur that is almost imperceptible at first, such as, for example, a change from the idea of revelation-over-reason to the idea of reason-over-revelation. However, with time, as the change becomes established in the sensibilities of the following generations, the effect of the change can be monumental.

Abstract Ideas

European philosophers, in a millennia long quest for certainty, have returned time and again to an idea about ideas, to wit: that certain ideas have a special status. What confers special status upon an idea is that it is a story about relationships that remain the same for all times, places, and peoples. "Logic," "geometry" and "mathematics" are words used to designate this type of narrative. Philosophers in the Western tradition have wanted to base their models of the circumstance on these ideas of special status. However, a question has to be asked: what can be said about such ideas *qua idea*? The answer is "not much." Take the idea of a triangle, an idea of special status made so because all triangles are always and everywhere the same (e.g., the interior angles of all triangles always add up to 180 degrees.) *Qua* idea, a triangle is a triangle in the same way that a stone by the side of the road is a stone by the side of the road. To be sure, a stone by the side of the road -- or the idea of a triangle -- -may be useful to human purpose, but a stone in and of itself is one of a vast number of objects by the side of the road, and a triangle in and of itself is one of a vast number of fixed relationships that can be established by carefully defining terms. In and of themselves stones and triangles *just are.*

Abstract ideas of any sort, from the idea of a triangle to the idea of God, **in order to be important in the life of a people,** have to be linked to human emotion. Such links are made in a way similar to (or perhaps identical with) the way that language is learned, i.e., as something acquired while growing up. What this means is that an abstract idea, in order to have meaning, purpose, or importance in human affairs, has to be based on narratives that are woven into the lives of a people and that are carried along by them from one generation to the next.

The crucial point to remember about stories based on abstract ideas -- God, nature, justice, reason, logic, evolution, triangles, 2+2=4 -- is that the emotional reactions that such stories engender are not the same for all peoples. No matter how unchanging and universal an idea may be, emotional reactions engendered by an abstract idea depend upon the history, temperament, intelligence, necessities, and grit of a particular people. The Egyptians, to take one example, used the idea of a three-four-five right triangle to establish property boundaries in the alluvial lands along the Nile River. However, they went no further. The Greeks, on the other hand, expanded the idea of a triangle into what they called "geometry," then expanded the idea of geometry into something that they called "the logos," then turned the idea of the logos into a worldview. Socrates came along and used the idea of the logos to try to change the mores and customs of the Athenians. Christians came along sometime later and turned the idea of the logos into an attribute of divinity. ("In the beginning was the *logos*.") Throughout the telling of all of these stories, the idea of a triangle *just was*. What made it more than a stone by the side of road was that it was incorporated into the narratives of various peoples in ways that were particular to them.

More narrative about the Second Synthesis

The Second Synthesis brought onto the stage of Europe a new type-man and a new type-woman. They were not lacking in virtues. Indeed, far from it. The best among them found ways to make wonderful contributions of every sort. With respect to even the best of Euro man and Euro woman of the Second Synthesis, however, problems existed. Their fundamental categories of us-and-them were based on antagonisms generated by activity in the political arena.

Why does it matter that their categories of "us" and "them" are determined by activity in the political arena?

All human communities have to carry out crucial tasks: courtship, forming a relationship with a member of the opposite sex, making babies, raising children, transmitting knowledge and values to the next generation, making a living, establishing viable forms of hierarchy, integration of male aggression into the community in a manner that steers between pusillanimity at one end and reduction of the landscape to rubble at the other, and much else. These tasks have to be accomplished in such a way that they lead to a coherent social order not once but over and over again down through the generations. For an action to be carried out over and over again, narratives have to be passed from one generation to the next that engender the emotions that issue forth into the actions that have to take place. To give this process a name, call it "tradition."

For centuries tradition shaped the sensibilities of the various peoples of and from Europe in ways that had a tendency to make the sensibilities of the population coherent. Men and men, men and women, children and adults, masters and servants came to have emotional reactions to each other that were complementary, thereby making it possible for them to live together and work with each other in some degree of harmony generation after generation.

Then change came to this European world. A new set of narratives emerged and became dominant, to wit: Second Synthesis stories about what OUGHT TO BE. The outcome was that over time these new stories replaced religion as the shaping force of sensibility. The process happened in stages. The first generations to be influenced by the new narrative of the Second Synthesis were men and women who as adolescents or as adults made a decision to embrace one or another of the new stories about how human life together OUGHT TO BE. Their decision expanded their worldview and gave them mental flexibility. Their *sensibilities*, however, were not formed by a new Second Synthesis story, but by the traditional, mainly religious stories of their youth. The result was that the people in the first generations of the Second Synthesis had minds made flexible by embracing new ideas, but morals and sensibilities established in them by the narratives of their Christian heritage. The combination was productive. The talented among the early generations of the Second Synthesis had brilliant careers and the creative among them made dazzling contributions.

However, the combination of flexible minds and traditional sensibilities did not last. The narratives of religion and of tradition lost vitality, stopped shaping the sensibilities of the rising generation, and were replaced by ideology, that is to say, by OUGHT TO BE stories of the Second Synthesis. The problem with ideology -- as narrative shaping sensibility -- is that it does not lead to a coherent social order. Under the influence of Second Synthesis stories, the social order fragmented and became post Babel. The cumbersome procedures and constraints of tradition gave way to an ever more disruptive recourse to *direct action*, i.e., to strikes, work stoppages, bribes, corruption, crime, blackmail, false flag events, and assassinations.

The glorious days are now gone when European peoples had the mental flexibility of new ideas and the morals and sensibilities of their Christian heritage. In the post Babel world of the present age, a type-man has risen to prominence, the psychopath, a man of no scruples and no remorse. He comes in two versions, strong leader and weak follower. The trait that defines the strong leader is a willingness to kill for money and power. The trait that defines the weak follower is an inclination to fawn upon the strong and to treat those lower in the social order with insolence and brutality. The strong leader wants power. To acquire it he will do whatever he can get away with. The weak follower wants permission to brutalize people who are in no position to strike back. These two type-men have complementary sensibilities and together they are able to create a stable social order. The order that they create, however – a mafia or a mafia-like gang -- is located on the bottom rung of the ladder of human life together.

The Enlightenment

Under the influence of changes caused by the so-called enlightenment, European intellectuals came to think that scraping away the barnacles of tradition and sweeping aside the cobwebs of superstition would remove fetters on human intellect, which upon being removed would lead to a golden age of man. What these intellectuals accomplished was approximately the opposite of what they set out to do. Not all traditions were cobwebs and barnacles. Some served an important purpose: contain and channel human emotion without extirpating it.

Obviously, distinctions are necessary. To preserve every tradition would be madness. Nobody wants to go back to leeches and bloodletting. The problem with enlightenment intellectuals is that they lacked mental categories needed for discernment. They knocked out social supports indiscriminately, some of which turned out to be pillars holding up the building in which they were living. A bit more thought about which social supports were weight-bearing, and which were not would have been helpful. The problem is that some crucial supports are so close to us, so intimately part of our life together as a people, that their importance cannot be discovered until they are gone, at which time it is too late to reestablish what was undone or has been dissipated.

A Message from Cunning Nature

The drama of Europe, with its layers of history and its succession of type-men coming on stage one after the other, contains a message from Cunning Nature, which, although not hard to understand, is hard to accept. "*Work with me,*" She says, "*incorporate me into the succession of your generations. Do not try to circumvent me. I will not be denied. If you do not want me integrated into your sensibilities, fine, go ahead, be my guest, do your best to exclude me, but be well assured that instead of excluding me, you will get me in ways that you do not want to have me -- raw, crude and unelaborated.*"

Science

Our ancestors in Old Europe, via a heritage of social capital of the highest quality, created the narrative foundations of a social order in which there was a reasonably disciplined leadership, refined sensibilities, and creativity of the highest rank in art, music, literature, and philosophy. This same heritage of social capital in Old Europe also led to the most spectacular and consequential -- but also the most mechanical, plebian and least subtle -- of Europe's many accomplishments: science and technology. Europeans were dazzled by their science.

> "Nature and nature's law lay hid in night,
> God said let Newton be and all was light."
> (Alexander Pope)

The enterprise of science has impressive accomplishments, to be sure, yet even so questions have to be asked. Who decides in which direction the enterprise of science is going to go? Who benefits from science? Who is damaged? Who has first claim on new scientific knowledge? Above all, who is in a position to vet the vast enterprise of science?

To vet science requires knowledge of a particular sort. Call it "wisdom," which, of course, raises a question: what is wisdom? Answer: it is self-knowledge and self-discipline. Almost any honest or sincere story using the word "wisdom" is likely to be helpful, e.g., wisdom as good judgment, as integrity, as limits, et cetera. For wisdom to be able to vet the high prestige enterprise of science, however, the narratives that engender the emotions that lead to actions that are wise have to be established in sensibility and passed along from one generation to the next, a task not easy to accomplish in the present age. Science itself disrupts the transmission of the narratives of wisdom across the generations. To look at one example among many, consider the pill and other forms of birth control. What the pill does is de-link sex from reproduction, thereby making sexual relations a matter of individual choice rather than a matter in which the interests of the community -- transmitted via tradition and custom – have an influence upon the behavior of individuals. Science, in other words, creates knowledge that undermines the processes by which science itself can be vetted.

In our now post Babel world, what happens to the enterprise of science? Answer: the same thing that happens to the state. Both science and the state are captured by the psychopath and his gang. What this means is that the first and strongest claim to the knowledge of science falls into the hands of the crudest type-man that we European people have to offer. If you want to see where this has landed us, look around. The vast military industrial complex -- not to mention excursions into strange, dark places such as MK-Ultra or the Covid flu drama -- is where un-vetted science in the hands of psychopathology takes us.

Truth as Public Good

Orgeta notes that many a man has been willing to die while marching behind banners proclaiming that 2+2=5. Does this mean that the man believes that 2+2=5? Yes and no. His assertion is a bid for power, for which power he will risk his life and kill you if you oppose him. However, even so, he will be pragmatic. When confronted with a situation in which it matters what 2+2 actually adds up to, he will come up with the number 4. On the other hand, if children are taught from infancy that 2+2=5, they may well believe it and act on it, which will cause problems for them later in life.

I think that the best way to think about truth is to think of it as a commons – a public good, a space open to all -- sustained by discourse. The discourse that sustains truth is of immense value to the community. The problem is that it is fragile. Every single individual in the community has an incentive to game the system, that is, to use the forums where truth is established to tell lies that benefit his or her interests.

Truth Always Matters

Suppose that we come to believe that narrative X is true. (Christianity, for example). The belief that X is true engenders emotions that lead to actions. These actions over time lead to a social order. Now suppose that the world changes again and doubts about narrative X begin to circulate. We might cherish X and want to preserve the social order that emerged because of its influence, but even so, if we come to harbor doubts about narrative X, our emotions will change, which change will lead to a change of action whether we want it to occur or not. One possible action that we could take, once doubts about X begin circulating, would be to discard X immediately. However, such a straightforward response rarely happens. All too often money, power, or established hierarchical relationships are at stake. As a result, doubts about X may lead to an elaborate re-telling of the story of X, or to attempts to maintain X by political correctness or going further still, by attempts to maintain X by coercion and violence.

Life, however, does not stand still. It falls into Hegelian patterns. A narrative defended by political correctness and violence develops a dialectic of its own. Honest people do not support a narrative in which they no longer believe, timid people keep a low profile (while watching which way the wind blows), and cagey people stay on board until a propitious moment arrives, at which time they abandon ship. Meanwhile, external opposition emerges and grows stronger. Sooner or later narrative X is replaced by narrative Y. This has to occur. There is no alternative. The process may be smooth, or difficult, or catastrophic, but it happens.

Evolution = Inequality

People of and from Europe have put a vast amount of effort into telling stories about equality and have undertaken a correspondingly vast amount of political activity based on such stories. In the present age a commitment to the idea of equality is a measure of moral seriousness. However, with respect to the concept, there is a problem. Equality does not exist. Nothing – looks, robustness, intelligence, stupidity, or anything else -- is handed out in equal measure, a truth so obvious that it has to be accommodated. Modern day, Second Synthesis, Euro people make the accommodation in a curious way. They change the unit of account. What starts as "all men are created equal" becomes "all groups are created equal," which represents retreat, but not far. Terrain conceded to inequality at the level of the individual is recovered by a fierce defense of equality at the level of the group. To say, hint, or suggest that some group is superior or inferior to some other group is the unpardonable *faux pas* of the present age.

We people of and from Europe, however, turn out to be wrong here, too. Nature stubbornly refuses to accommodate our notions about how life ought to be. Equality does not exist at the level of the group any more than it exists anywhere else. The response of Euro people to this un-cooperative tendency on the part of nature is to refuse to accept the data, or refuse to engage in debates about the data, or to lower the boom of social opprobrium on people who dare uncover and discuss the data.

Equality is anti-nature. Living creatures change and adapt to new conditions because some are in a better position to deal with the new conditions than others. Evolution = inequality. However, having said all of the above, let me now make the following assertion: there is a way in which **equality** is essential.

A Case for Equality

(a short dialogue in voices)

We human beings are flawed and contradictory creatures. Social altitude and power all too often make us arrogant and opaque to any truth that we do not like. Ah, but nothing is simple and straightforward. Social altitude also is necessary for us to have the confidence to see ourselves as we are and to impose discipline upon ourselves, which discipline is the *sine qua non* of leadership.

Are you saying that in order to have confidence there has to be inequality?

Yes, for confidence and for much else there has to be inequality. Equality is unworkable. "Take away but degree," says a character in one of Shakespeare's plays, "and hark, what discord follows."[56] This character is right.

I'm confused. If you believe that equality is unworkable, why are you now making a case for it?

Equality of a certain sort is possible, indeed necessary.

How so? In what way?

There can be an equality of manners, based on the chivalric code.

The chivalric code? What is that?

According to Edmund Burke, it is a code of behavior that makes "kings into companions;" that raises "private men to be fellows with kings," and that, "without confounding rank, produces a noble equality [that] is handed down through all the gradations of social life..." [57]

What did Burke mean?

He meant that an ordinary man cannot expect to be equal to a king, but an ordinary man can have the same manners and standards as a king. If the man fails to live up to the standards of the chivalric code, he is judged to be inadequate. Ah, but so too is a king judged to be inadequate if **he** fails to live up to the standards of the chivalric code. Here there is equality. King and commoner

[56] Shakespeare, *Troilus and Cressida,* act 1, scene 3, lines 112-13.
[57] [Burke, *Reflections on the Revolution in France,* Penguin books, p.170].

are measured by the same yardstick, especially in crucial matters having to do with valor.

Maybe you have not noticed a small detail. We don't have kings anymore, except in some places where to encourage tourism they linger on as state-sponsored soap opera.

We have rank and always will.

Oh, come on, "the chivalric ideal!" You can't be serious? You are just saying words –archaic words, as a matter of fact.

Of course I am just saying words. What are any of us but the words that we say, the emotions that our words engender in us, and the actions that we take based on the emotions that our words cause us to feel?

What is the point that you are trying to make?

Equality of one particular sort is possible, an equality of manners. It is in fact the only sort of equality that is possible. To achieve an equality of manners, however, we have to have a social order that respects gradations of rank. Only an elite with vision and *esprit de corps* has the discipline to hold **itself** to high standards and the confidence to hold the rest of us to the same high standards as well.

You live in a strange world. Equality leads to a post Babel takeover of the state by psychopaths, who soon turn everybody into slaves except for a few henchmen. On the other hand, done right, inequality leads to an equality of manners that spreads down through the gradations of society, thereby making people equal in the crucial realm of manners and valor.

Yes, well said. This is correct.

A Letter to Our Women

Dear Women,

We men and women of and from Europe have created a mess that has to be cleaned up. To clean it up requires telling stories. The story that I am going to tell now begins back in hunter-gathering times, in a setting in which all of us, you women and we men, are sitting around a campfire. In this setting we are together, but each of us has our own sphere of influence. Yours is the space around the campfire; ours is out in the wilderness beyond the campfire.

Drawing the attention of you women in your sphere of interest are matters having to do with children, food, manners, relationships, the aesthetics of campfire life, hierarchy, etc. The power that you have is the power of peer pressure and social coercion. Although we men are deeply interested in what happens around the campfire, our identity hinges on events that occur in the wilderness among ourselves and among alien men against whom we are arrayed. Stripped of cant and euphemism, the power that we men have is the power to kill (prey animals, rivals, enemies). Derivative of our power to kill is the power to establish hierarchies among ourselves. What this means is that we men have to have sufficient emotional intensity to let ourselves see danger, act with courage in the face of danger, and risk being killed. The high degree of emotional intensity required for us to carry out our various tasks is what is meant by the word "vitality."

The roles that we men and women play and the various emotions that we feel influence our lives together. As a rule, drawing us to you women is your health and beauty. On the other hand, what draws you women to us is our vitality. The pattern of men being drawn to beauty and of women being drawn to vitality emerged in hunter-gathering times, lasted through the age of agriculture, and is still with us today. However, the pattern is causing problems in the present age. You women now see yourselves as a separate group *vis-à-vis* us and you tell stories about how you have been relegated by us to an inferior status. In addition to seeing yourselves as victims, you also see various other people as victims, which people you consider to be your allies. The vision that animates the stories that you tell is one in which everybody is sitting around the campfire as equals. To give a label to your vision, call it "radical inclusiveness."

Emotions engendered by your vision of radical inclusiveness are not superficial. They trace back to the time when we men had to be high-strung in order to carry out our various tasks. In a world of high-strung men, you women invariably found yourselves acting as peacemakers and shock absorbers, doing your best to keep us men from exploding into violence among ourselves. To preserve harmony around the campfire is a desire that is deeply ingrained in you.

About you women, however, it is necessary to say more. There is an aspect of life that can be classified under the heading of the word "power." This aspect of life – this thing called "power" -- you like as much as we men do. How you acquire power is via peer pressure and social coercion. This is normal. This is what you do. This is what you have always done. Such activity on your part is an essential component of our lives together as a people. The problem we have with you women is not that you use peer pressure and social coercion to acquire power, but the stories in the service of which you now deploy your power. Your story about radical inclusiveness works for you. It gives you a very high moral-high-ground from which to deploy your capacity to exert peer pressure and social coercion. However, your story does not work for us. It is a dagger to the heart. The source of the problem that we have with your story is biology. The genes and allels that make us men who we are have to pass through your wombs. Were you to realize your project of radical inclusiveness, we would lose control of your wombs. This is not trivial. Who you mate with is an issue of vital concern to us. If you mate with men unlike ourselves, we Euro men within a few generations would cease to exist as a unique creation of nature.

Do you understand the importance of this point. Strong forces are at work. The basic, fundamental game of life is in play.

Were we men to acquiesce to your project of radical inclusiveness, we would have to suppress the drive in ourselves to recreate ourselves in the next generation, a drive that lies at the heart of life and is deeply intwined with passion, action, vitality, confidence, and power. Suppressing this drive would lead to a loss of confidence, of vitality, and of *esprit de corps* on our part. Do you understand the implications of this point? Your project of radical inclusiveness, were it to be successful, would turn us into demoralized men. Ah, but what are demoralized men to you? The answer is this: they are men who **as men** are of no interest to you **as women**?

On the other hand, if we resist your project, the view that you have of yourselves as victims would be confirmed. You would continue doing what you are doing now – would you not – that is, work yourselves into a state of high dudgeon, mount a drama of good guy versus bad guy, and assign to us the role of bad guy?

You see our dilemma? Your project of radical inclusiveness leaves us either disdained **by** you (because you consider us to be wimps) or alienated **from** you (because you consider us to be male chauvinists). Surely, we together – who are the flesh of each other's flesh and the blood of each other's blood -- can do better than that.

In the split that has emerged between us, which party is correct? Are you women correct in thinking that we men should overcome proclivities formed in us over the millennia of the deep past and join with you in your project of universal inclusiveness? Or, on the other hand, should we men work with nature and **not** force ourselves to lie down in a bed of Procrustes based on your current notions about what OUGHT TO BE.

Not surprisingly, I take the side of men.

In my opinion you women are not creating a social order based on a vision of radical inclusiveness. What is happening is darker and more sinister. You are letting yourself be used by our rivals. If you doubt me, ask this question: where does your narrative about radical inclusiveness come from? The *causa remota* of your narrative is the fragmentation of the Second Synthesis, which has led us, we men and you women, to form ourselves into separate groups, each with our own narratives. The *causa proxima* of your narrative, on the other hand, are the men of the deep state who are using their control of the media to circulate your stories about radical inclusiveness. Please understand, they circulate these stories **not** because they want everybody to sit together in harmony around the campfire, but because they want to demoralize us, we men of and from Europe, so that they can prevail over us in the political arena. What they are doing is not *Kumbaya, my Lord*, but political combat dressed in the garb of high morality.

These men of the deep state are, in effect, making you an offer: "give us state power and we will help you realize your project of radical inclusiveness," they say. "If problems arise, we will protect you via laws, jobs, bureaucracies, subsidies, and control of the narrative. You can count on us. We will be your men."

Their offer touches emotions in you that go deep. They are offering three outcomes that you want: life around the campfire made harmonious, emotional links to vital men (i.e., to men such as they are), and a very high moral high ground to stand on (to deploy your powers of social coercion). Understand, however, an important point. Their offer is not sincere. They want to damage us, we men of and from Europe. In so far as you go along with them, you are contributing to their intent. It appears, however, that these men of the deep state do not bother you. You seem to be unaware of their psychopathology, perhaps because you are attracted to (what you take to be) their vitality.

However, even so, having said all the above, let me make the following point: in your emotional responses to these men, I sense **not** malevolence on your part so much immaturity. For all your talk about power in relationships between men and women, there is something in your emotional responses to the men at the top of the state that is childlike. You do not ask a critical question: "where are they taking us?" The answer is that they are taking you women to a place where men manipulate men, where men dominate men, and where from time-to-time men kill men. That is, they are taking you to the political arena. I am not saying that you should avoid being drawn into the political arena, but I am saying this: if you bring a childlike credulity to the political arena, you will be co-opted in the blink of an eye.

The hope I have for you women is that you become more self-aware. Do not buy what the psychopaths are selling. They want to degrade our communities in order to consolidate power in **their** hands (not yours and certainly not in ours). Before you ally yourselves with them, consider a counteroffer from us. Be our women, become our partners, anchor our families, support our communities, deploy your talent for peer pressure and social coercion in an alliance with us. When we are too violent, use your influence to pull us back. When we are too timid, become Valkyries exhorting us to man-up. We can be bullies without you and we can be slaves without you, but we cannot attain the highest expression of what it means to be a man without you.

The way that we people of and from Europe now live lacks continuity. Each generation has to start over again from zero. No accumulation of wisdom occurs. Would you not prefer to live in a community in which *esprit de corps*, good manners, refined taste, valor, vitality, and beauty build upon themselves? In the not too distant past, we European peoples created communities in which what was good about us built upon itself. The problem is that we did so in ways that were marred by illusion, by lack of self-knowledge, and by error. However, we can learn from the past -- can we not -- and find ways to go down the road with an increase of intentionality, however modest the increase might be? I say that, yes, this is possible. I invite you to join us in creating communities in which narratives about valor, nobility, and beauty influence how we organize our lives together. This is the future for us, if we as a people have one.

Sincerely yours,

Your faithful other

A Letter to Men of and from Europe.

Dear Euro men,

Due to the exigencies of history and evolution, our women now find purpose and a sense of power by inviting everybody to join them around the campfire. If they are successful, we men will be dissolved into an ocean of undifferentiated humanity and disappear as a unique creation of nature. To continue to exist as unique creatures, we are going to have to win our women back. It won't be easy. Look at us now – especially at those of us in the United States -- and tell me what you see. I'll tell you what I see, an unattractive group of overweight, vulgar, conformist, demoralized men who are afraid of being called names, who lack *esprit de corps*, who do not care about the past or the future of their own people, and who have no map to guide them through the currents of life except fad, fashion, and stories told to them by men who hate them. As if not already bad enough, when I look at us, I see men who consider the following to be acceptable:

* that it is okay for foreigners to colonize our homelands;
* that we cannot live in neighborhoods restricted to people like ourselves *if we want to*;
* that we cannot send our children to schools with people like themselves *if we want to*;
* that we have to hire people unlike ourselves even if we do not want to do so;
* that we cannot discuss among ourselves topics of vital interest to us (e.g., the truth or not of the Holocaust, black IQ, our evolution as a species) without facing peer pressure and social coercion in all of the countries in which we live and legal sanctions in some of the countries in which we live;
* that we think that laws legally discriminating against us in favor of black people (and now foreigners) are okay;

* that we are afraid to apply to black people, to foreigners, and to Jews the morals, manners, and standards of conduct that we apply to ourselves.

What woman would want the sort of men that we have turned ourselves into? Out of resignation or ignorance or desperation or because she herself is demoralized, a woman might accept such a man as we have become, but we are not what she wants.

To win back our women is a task of the highest importance. Required to accomplish this task is *not* that we become less -- but rather that we become more -- manly. Understand, manliness does not mean pushing weak people around. Rather it means making demands upon ourselves to become more disciplined, accomplished, respectful, moral, witty, vital, dangerous -- and not fat. Manliness does not mean that we proclaim loudly how great we are, but with good manners show how determined we are. Manliness does not involve killing people who present no threat to us (to prove to ourselves that we are men) and it certainly does not mean killing people for Israel. However, manliness does mean that we resist people who DO present a threat to us. It means that we are tough and aggressive when trenched upon. Above all it means that when in the course of human events it becomes necessary for us to defend ourselves, we are ready, no matter from where the threat appears, whether from discourse, economics, politics, social coercion, peer pressure, or violence.

It would be nice if we could count upon our women to help us recover our manhood, but we cannot. To make ourselves into men is not their job. It is ours. Their job is to choose winners. Our job is to be a winner. It is that simple.

The Deep State

The men who I define as "The Worst" have created the deep state. This state operates behind a façade of hollowed out Second Synthesis institutions. The men of the deep state make the rules (the real rules, you understand, the ones that are enforced). They are strong, these men. The source of their strength is violence dished out with impunity. Their strength, however, is also their weakness. They have no vision. Their court of highest appeal is not a moral or spiritual narrative, but power. The simplicity of their strategy -- power at any cost -- gives them clarity, and clarity makes them strong. Their strength, however, is the strength of glass, unyielding yet brittle. One blow delivered in the right way shatters them.

While the Worst have no moral or spiritual court of highest appeal, they do have an effective tactic: Gramsci's march though the institutions. To capture one institution after another works for them. It is a strategy, however, that does not work for us. The incentive structure is wrong. In the large sovereign units in which most of us now live, all roads lead to fascism, that is, to a polity in which the power of government, finance, and industry funnel down into the hands of a reduced number of people. In such a polity, psychopaths win most of the battles.

We are not going to prevail in a struggle to capture the state as it is now constituted. The writ of the authority of the contemporary state encompasses too many different peoples, too much territory, and too many different type-men. In our big, sprawling, sovereign units, one outcome is inevitable: capture of the sovereignty of the state by a small, cohesive group. And indeed, this has happened. In the case of the so-called United States, the men now dominant are Jews. That they sit at the top of the political mountain was not inevitable. However, that *some* smaller, more cohesive group would capture the state *was* inevitable. Jews turned out to be a competent gang that got there first.

Capture of the state by a gang or tribe is not a side issue or an incidental problem. On the contrary, it is the crucial issue of our age. How do we deal with it?

A March Overland through the Counties.

Movement for us cannot be vertical (up or down through the institutions). Rather, it has to be horizontal (overland through the counties), which means capturing territory bit by bit and decentralizing the institutions found therein. Take schools as a small but useful example. There should be no centrally located primary schools, but rather, many neighborhood schools, or perhaps even a single house in each neighborhood converted into a school for the children of that particular neighborhood. The reason for a high level of disaggregation is obvious. Primary schools should be within walking distance for most children; teachers should live in the same neighborhood as their students; and children should go to school with their own kind. (It is not the job of children to solve problems of "diversity" that adults have been unable to solve since time immemorial.) The same consideration applies to high schools -- not one big one but many small ones -- for the same reason: it is easier for Zionists, politicians, unions, and bureaucrats to capture a single big school than it is for them to capture many smaller ones.

Making institutions local and independent is a pattern to apply not just to schools but across the board to manufacturing, to retail, and above all to banking. Commerce and finance, when consolidated into big, nation-wide corporations, are easier to be captured by small, cohesive groups. Not so long ago a bank could only operate within a banking district which was quite small. We have to apply this pattern not just to banking but to all commerce, including the big franchise operations that now mar our physical, social, moral and aesthetic landscape. Perhaps some loss of economic efficiency would ensue were big, nationwide franchise operations to be reined in. However, any loss would more than be compensated for by gains in the quality of men and women who would emerge among us. There would also be an increase in the degree of liberty that we would come to enjoy. (Liberty = the space that exists legally and socially between what is forbidden and what is mandatory).

Neo-Contractarianism

Fragmentation within the sovereign unit leads to consolidation of government. Diversity – within a sovereign unit -- is the strength of government. Diversity **of** sovereign units is the health of a people. Given that we live in big sovereign units, what should we do? First and foremost: recognize the gravity of the problem. Second, have the confidence to speak among ourselves with candor and honesty. Third, take recourse in a strategy that can be called "neo-contractarianism," understood as follows: we agree among ourselves to live by a set of rules that structure our political lives. Yes, yes, I know, far from being new, this is standard, off-the-shelf, garden variety Contract Doctrine. What makes it "neo" is as follows: not everybody is invited to join the rule making assembly. Restrictions are placed on who may attend the constitutional convention where the rules are decided upon. To speak bluntly but candidly, no blacks, Jews, or foreigners can have input into decisions about *how* we organize ourselves and about *who* our leaders are (in return for which we abjure having input into the selection of their leaders and their rules). We become Amish after a fashion and start creating politically separate communities (even if we continue to live within the same geographic area). In effect, we go into internal exile, as the Amish have done, and start the process of reversing "diversity" at the micro level step by step.

Think of neo-contractarianism is a tourniquet applied to stop bleeding -- **ours.** What is going to be hard to do for those of us who live in the USA is discard the Philadelphia constitution of 1789, but discard it we must. This document is now a hindrance. The men of deep state are skilled at conforming to the letter of the constitution while violating its spirit. If the pretense of having a constitution were discarded, the men of the deep state would have to walk naked before us. As for us, each one of us would have to look into the mirror and ask a very personal question: "do I want to be slave?" As matters now stand, the letter of the law *observed* gives us a pretext to avoid having to face the spirit of the law *violated*.

I understand, of course, that by the reckoning of the present age, to organize ourselves into smaller, more homogeneous units, and to begin reversing the tyranny of diversity, would be called anti-Semitism, racism, white supremacy, etc., all of which is the bread and butter of political combat and entirely to be expected. My purpose in writing these essays is not to convince blacks and Jews to become more like us, or to try to convince them to start treating us with respect. Rather, my purpose is to encourage us, we men of and from Europe, to overcome our demoralization and get back into the game of life. The day we begin acting like men is the day that they will begin treating us with respect.

We now lack the wisdom, training, discipline, confidence, and leadership needed to deal with Jews, blacks, and foreigners in a polity in which truth is NOT the highest court of appeal. Were these various peoples willing to deal with us in the currency of truth, then perhaps some kind of viable *convivencia* (life together) might be possible. Their refusal to deal in the currency of truth, however, is a problem. We men of and from Europe do not now have the solidarity and courage needed to counter the cohesion, the hypocrisy, and the gangster tactics of the Jews, nor do we know how to resist the violence and indiscipline of the blacks, nor can we resist the relentless pressure upon us coming from people living in countries that are overpopulated. We lack the confidence and the courage that we have to have to defend ourselves even in our own homelands. We European peoples need to start the long process of recovering what has been lost, which turns out to be just about everything, e.g., élan, *esprit de corps*, manhood, confidence, morality, beauty, high art, and control of our own destiny.

Free Speech and the Composition of the Sovereign Unit

We who live in the United States have a document, the constitution of 1789, the first amendment of which states that there are to be no laws abridging the freedom of speech. This amendment is now under pressure. Informal (social) restrictions on everyday speech are creeping upward into the realm of law and government. The problem is diversity (within the sovereign unit). It exists. It is real. We human creatures are different and these differences are hard to deal with. The people who say that "diversity is our strength" are asserting that 2+2=5. They assert it because it makes it easier for them to consolidate power at top of the state. They do not practice it among themselves.

We people (of and from Europe) have serious conflicts of interest with blacks, with Jews, and now with foreigners. These differences, however, we do not discuss openly and candidly because we sense – accurately, I think – that the differences are too acute to be talked about without destabilizing the system. Restraint on our part translates into political power on their part. However, the process is breaking down. Their power is now so pronounced that it is becoming dangerous. They do not want speech to be uncensored because they do not want the real, serious conflicts of interest that divide us to become acceptable topics of political debate.

With respect to laws like the first amendment, there comes a moment of insight. Uncensored speech is not possible in polities where differences among groups are too acute to be talked about. In such a polity, the only way that issues can be resolved is by dishonesty, or control of the media, or corruption, or intimidation, or violence. An unpalatable truth has to be faced. It is not possible to create a political entity and then pass laws that guarantee free speech. This formula does not work. It is like thinking that in a polity of English-speaking people you can pass a law that requires everybody to speak Latin. It can be done, but would take generations and require a very strong authority.

If you want uncensored speech, you have to start with a group of people who are capable of sustaining forums among themselves in which truth is the highest court of appeal. The mistake of the Founding Fathers was to think that uncensored speech could be sustained by words written on a piece of paper. This is error. Uncensored speech depends on matters deeply rooted in the customs, history, and temperament of a people.

The Journey of Discover Undertaken by Our Political Class

With the decline of a confident aristocracy and with the loss of vitality of the Christian religion, our politicians lost whatever (shaky) control as moral agents that they had over themselves. However, in the general population, traditional Christian morality continued to be vital for a few more generations, which meant that if a politician infracted a stricture of morality (such as getting a divorce), consequences would ensue that he would feel. Ah, but history does not stop. It keeps rolling along. The population has now caught up with the political class, one consequence of which is that constraints on politicians now depend less on morals and manners and more on the crude mechanism of law, a change that gives to the political class more latitude of action. They, after all, have much control over the law and its application. However, even so, be this as it may, it was not clear to the political class just how much latitude of action they actually enjoyed. As a result, much about recent history can be thought of as involving a journey of discovery undertaken by the political class to answer this question: "how much can we get away with?"

The answer turns out to be **a lot.**

Start with Franklin Roosevelt. He wanted a war and worked assiduously to gin one up. It is very likely that he had knowledge of the imminent attack on Pearl Harbor, but did not inform his commander in Hawaii. He thought (correctly as it turned out) that an attack on Pearl Harbor would lead to the war that he wanted.

Next consider political murders of Americans committed by American politicians. Among such crimes were some of the most consequential events in 20th century American history, e.g., the murder of James Forrestal, of John Kennedy, of Robert Kennedy, and of Martin Luther King. Another series of stops on this journey of discovery can be classified under the heading of false flag attacks, e.g., Operation Gladio, the Oklahoma City bombing, 9/11, probably Sandy Hook, and who knows what else? Next consider the phony attack in the Gulf of Tonkin, a lie used to justify a war in Viet Nam. Two generation later another lie – this time about "weapons of mass destruction" -- was used to gin up a war in Iraq. As we come down to the present, do not relax. The journey is not over. Ukraine is the current port of call. The war taking place there now was ginned up by the government entity in Washington, in what has to be considered one the most callous, brutal, and cynical events in the history of our country. What makes the war in Ukraine unique is not that it was unnecessary – all of them have been unnecessary -- but that it blocked a healthy development. The Russians wanted to participate in commerce with the European Union and would have added to the prosperity of all. However, the neo-cons and other psychopaths in Washington would have none of it. Their intransigence, stupidity, ambition, psychopathology, and narcissism led to the current debacle in Ukraine, a truly dark, dark enterprise. If future generations have the leisure to contemplate the part of *their* past that is *our* present, they will consider the decision to gin up a war in Ukraine, made by the Washington entity, to be a monument to human depravity.

Most Americans and Europeans do not want to know about this sordid journey of discovery undertaken by their political class. They see the state as a daddy to be relied upon. Their belief in the state acts as a sort of magic dust, which upon being sprinkled around, causes the crimes of the political class not to disappear or to be forgotten, but to be explained away by transparent, self-serving lies. However, all is not lost. Truth has a certain staying power.

Truth Lags Events
Sensibility Lags Truth

History does not stop. It rolls along generation after generation, one consequence of which is that young people are always arriving on the scene with sensibilities in the process of being formed. Does this have an effect? I say that yes, it does. The rising generation exerts a pressure towards truth. To explain what I mean, let me (as usual) set up a model, in this case one with five steps.

Step 1. Choose one event to investigate. The one I choose for this exercise is 9/11.

Step 2. Set up a model. Mine is this: granite surrounded by sedimentary rock. That's it. That's the entire model. Granite = truth. Sedimentary rock = error, propaganda, lies, and deception. The model assumes that as time passes the weaker sedimentary rock erodes faster than the granite, leaving more granite (i.e., more truth) exposed.

Step 3. Divide the population into three cohorts. A = those who do not think about or care about 9/11. B = those who are perpetrators, supporters, and beneficiaries of 9/11. C = those who want to know the truth.

Step 4. To crank the model, start with group A (those who do not care). The members of this group absorb bits and pieces of the official story, but remain inert unless a new consensus emerges. They are essentially irrelevant.

Go next to Group B (perps and beneficiaries). This group will not initiate debate about 9/11. They want the official narrative to be accepted, not looked at nor talked about. If you challenge the official narrative, however, they will attack, which attack will be deployed in stages, starting with *ad hominem* name calling, then escalating upward through peer pressure, social coercion, economic pressure (loss of job, of income, etc.), violence, and finally as a last resort, in crucial cases, murder. Members of Group B will not go near the granite of truth. They themselves do not want to think about the facts of 9/11 and most certainly they do not want us to think about the facts.

Then there is group C, those who care about truth. The members of this group want to know what happened. Their focus is upon the granite, i.e., known facts, science, eyewitness accounts, explanations that fit what was happening before the event and afterwards, and above all upon *cui bono*. The books that they write will be as factual and as plausible as they can make them. My conclusion is that Group C will have a disproportionate influence upon the formation of sensibility among young people of the rising generations, especially as the perpetrators grow old and die off.

Step 5. Conclusions. Because of group C, facts, scientific relationships, eyewitness accounts, and *cui bono* will have more influence as time passes. Lies and deception, on the other hand, will seem contrived, *ad hoc,* and unconvincing. The conclusion that I draw is that there is a tendency for truth to emerge as time passes and then, once it does, there is a tendency for it to influence the sensibilities of the rising generation. I am sure that glaring exceptions to this conclusion can be found, but overall, it seems reasonable to think that -- sooner or later, most of the time, in one way or the other -- truth arrives on stage and has at least some influence upon sensibility.

The time is out of joint. O cursèd spite, that ever I was born to set it right! [58]

We have a super-abundance of evidence that the time is out of joint and like Hamlet we dither. However, I disagree with Hamlet on one point. To set matters right is not a curse. On the contrary, it is a task that gives to our lives meaning and purpose. In that sense the task is a gift, though admittedly one that is hard to appreciate when the deep state is bestowing upon us its favors.

The sordid truth about the Washington entity will emerge. As it does, sensibility will follow and put pressure on the psychopaths in power. They will try to shift responsibility away from themselves, which, however, will not be easy to do. So brutal, so callous, so dark, so counterproductive, so stupid, yet so inter-connected,

---

[58] Shakespeare, *Hamlet*, Act 1, scene 5 lines 187-8

transparent, and ugly is the truth about the Washington entity, that half-measures and partial revelations are unlikely to be successful. A "limited hangout" – i.e., a partial revelation of truth while retaining control of the narrative and of the legal apparatus of the state – will not work. The tide of truth, once it starts flowing, will become a flood. To maintain their power, the men of the deep state will have to climb the ladder of repression.

Rungs on the ladder of repression:

1) Propaganda, lies, name calling, social coercion.
2) Blackmail, bribes, corruption.
3) Swat teams kicking down doors at 6 a.m. with a servile press in tow.
4) Law-fare, the corrupt use of the legal apparatus of the state for the purpose of directing the violence of the state against political opponents.
5) Assassinations and crimes carried out with "plausible deniability." (Keep in mind that the purpose of "plausible deniability" is not to cover up a crime. Knowledgeable people usually have a good idea about who is behind a political crime, or at least what interests are behind it. Charles de Gaulle, for example, upon hearing about the assassination of Kennedy, is reported to have said that the Americans would not find out who did it, that they did not want to know. Exactly. The purpose of "plausible deniability" is to give people who do not want to know a reason not to look.)
6) Shooting people retail in the street.
7) Killing people wholesale out of sight.
8) Gulags and terror as government policy.

Dear Men of and from Europe: how far they go up the ladder of repression depends on us. Be prepared to "cavil on the ninth part of a hair" and resist them every step of the way.

Sincerely,

Your faithful correspondent

Sovereignty and Culture

(a Last Dialogue in Voices)

Sovereignty is a term used to define a political entity in which some men have the right to kill other men with impunity (declare war, execute criminals, kill people who become violent, et cetera).

Presumably the right to kill with impunity can only be invoked under well-defined conditions.

Yes, of course, but you are assuming that those who have the right to kill with impunity can be compelled to stay within limits.

This is hard to do?

Yes.

What's the problem?

The glue that holds our big sovereign units together loses cohesiveness with the passage of time. Meanwhile groups inside the sovereign unit become better organized and more tightly linked. Fragmentation is the inevitable outcome. The process begins with bureaucrats who see themselves as entitled. It reaches a middle stage when politics devolves into a contest to capture the institutions of the state. The end is reached when a gang positions itself at the point of maximum power, which is to be inside the state, but outside the law.

What is culture?

It is art, literature, customs, information of a useful or scientific nature, and just about anything else of interest. However, culture also has another meaning. It refers to relationships among a people. We sometimes say about a people that they share the same culture. What this means is that the stories that they tell, the emotions that they feel, and the actions that they take tend to fall within the same general range.

What is the point that you want to make about culture and sovereignty?

We have a tendency to associate only with people who live with us inside our sovereign unit and who share with us the same or a similar culture. This is natural and healthy. We can, however, under the right conditions, include the narratives and culture from other sovereign units made up of people who are unlike us.

How so? What are you saying?

Think of what I am suggesting here as a way to approximate, however crudely, the early stages of the Second Synthesis, when we had the mental flexibility of new ideas, and the social cohesion made possible by having still vital moral strictures from out Christian past.

Small, homogeneous sovereign units, besides providing the best protection against capture by psychopaths, gangs, or tribes, have a better chance of establishing viable moral and social frameworks in terms of which to understand and conduct the affairs of the collective.

You seem to want lots of smaller units of sovereignty?

Yes, I do.

This means that you want to break up the big countries in which most of us people in and from Europe now live?

Yes, I do.

...including your own country, the United States...?

Especially my own country.

I had a feeling that you were heading in this direction. Once again, as with your ideas about monarchy, I think that you are indulging in fantasy. The attempt to break up your country has already been tried. It didn't work then. What makes you think that it will work now?

The government of the big, heterogeneous American nation has turned out to be an easy target for organized subgroups to capture. Where these subgroups are taking us is not pretty to contemplate.

Where is it that they are taking us?

Our government corrupted, our land degraded, our cities ugly, our morals vulgar, our population dumbed-down, our foreign policy brutal (and hugely counterproductive to our interests), our art hideous, our finances in disarray, and what remains of our patriotism exploited to fight destructive, unnecessary wars at the behest of a foreign power -- this is where they are taking us. The wreck that is the Washington government does not merit lasting one minute longer than it takes to break it up.

You really think that the status quo is so bad that the United States should be dismembered?

Yes. European nations in general and the United States in particular have lost authority. The governments of these countries are facades behind which criminality runs riot. Had we the valor of our ancestors, we long ago would have consigned the lot of them to the trash heap of history.

If breaking up the United States of America is your solution, you don't have one. A breakup is not going to happen.

Don't be so sure. Sixty-nine years after *The Communist Manifesto* came out in 1848, the Marxists got themselves a state. It took a while, but they did it.

What would you like to see happen?

I would like to see the emergence of a contemporary version of Old Europe, a second growth Old Europe, made up of smaller, more homogeneous sovereign units led by men linked to us by genetics and shared history. As was the case in Old Europe, I would like for there to be rich and varied contacts of culture among the various sovereign units. Diversity is of great benefit if we have a secure foundation of sovereignty from which to assimilate -- or reject -- cultural influences coming from other peoples.

You want to re-create by intention what European peoples stumbled into by the accidental confluence of genetics, geography and history.

Yes.

How small do you want the sovereign units to be?

Size depends on three considerations that are local: geography, culture, and ethnicity; and one consideration that is general: the technology of war. Our sovereign units have to be big enough to afford weapons that make the cost of attacking us high. A fact of history working in our favor is that it is becoming cheaper to create weapons of vast lethality. To be dangerous, we do not have to be big.

You are beginning to sound like a crank on a soapbox telling stories about what OUGHT TO BE?

Good point. Guilty as charged, except that I plead that I am not telling just another, OUGHT TO BE story. About my narrative I claim that 1) it is not utopian, 2) it is not sentimental, 3) it aspires to work with -- not circumvent – nature, 4) it makes an attempt to think about what made Old Europe successful, and 5) it makes an attempt to think about what went wrong with Old Europe. Oh, in addition, there is one other point. I invite you to judge the validity of my story not just by what I advocate but also by what I jettison.

What do you jettison?

The idea of reason as a unique quality of mind and the idea that contractarian discourse about equality and justice can form the basis of a stable life together.

What would we accomplish were we to get rid of these narratives?

We would put ourselves in a better position to see what we are now skilled at finding ways **not** to see: the abysmal failure of the nation states that we have built for ourselves.

Are you proclaiming the death of the nation state?

No, but I am proclaiming the death of the nation state as **dinosaur**. If we European peoples have a future, it will be in small sovereign units that are supportive of our interests as a people and that are much more attuned to the rhythms of nature. Sovereignty in the next age will **not** be a clumsy reptile, but a graceful mammal.

What Yucatan asteroid is going to usher in the transition from reptile to mammal?

I don't know, but we will find out. To steal a line from Soren Kierkegaard, I think that there will come a time when our soul will be required of us.

The End

Paul C. Johnston

Contact the author at:
paulclark749@gmail.com

www.ingramcontent.com/pod-product-compliance
Lightning Source LLC
LaVergne TN
LVHW090607110826
845146LV00001B/296

* 9 7 9 8 9 9 3 4 9 3 6 0 2 *